CW00666549

Praise for Euban
Artificial Intelligence fc

"HR professionals need to unc changing while helping employees develop and prioritize the skills they will need for the age of disruption, and Ben Eubanks' take on how we can combine humans and technology paints a bright picture for the future of the HR profession."
Mary Kaylor, Corporate Communications Manager, Robert Half

"In this must-read book, [Eubanks] presents the contemporary and very real challenges of artificial intelligence that will change not only how we look at the world of work, but also how we approach what we do in the workplace every day."
Dr. Kim LaFevor, Senior Executive of Strategy and Innovation, Athens State University

"If you are in search of a data-packed, transformational book, I'd encourage you to take the time to dive deep, take notes, and transform your own business with what you learn."
Trent Cotton, VP Talent and Culture, HatchWorks

"Today's experience-driven employer relationship requires a keen focus on the individual. As Ben Eubanks' book demonstrates, AI technologies are going to help HR leaders personalize the employee experience and create more human relationships in powerful, scalable ways."
China Gorman, Board Chair, Human Resources Certification Institute (HRCI)

"HR leaders must understand technology to thrive in the modern business environment and AI is one of the most transformational technologies of our age... [Eubanks] simplifies the complexity of AI and highlights pragmatic opportunities for every HR function. It's a must-read for any HR professional looking to thrive in today's disruptive environment."
Christopher Lind, Chief Learning Officer, ChenMed and Founder, Learning Sharks

Other books by Ben Eubanks:

Artificial Intelligence for HR (2018)
Artificial Intelligence for HR, *2nd Edition* (2022)

ISBN (paperback): 9798374890334

Talent
Scarcity

How to
Hire and Retain
a Shrinking Workforce

Ben Eubanks

DEDICATION

To my father, who uses an increasingly rare set of skills every
day to solve problems that make others quit.

You taught me to think around challenges,
work harder when others quit,
and care deeply about the people I serve,
both at work and at home.

ACKNOWLEDGMENTS

It's often been said:

If you want to go fast, go alone. If you want to go far, go together.

Thanks to Melanie, Joe, George, Jacki, and the others who
have played a part in helping me to go far. I'm beyond
thankful and blessed to know each one of you.

ABOUT THE AUTHOR

Ben Eubanks is a writer, speaker, and researcher living in Huntsville, Alabama. His work has been featured in numerous industry publications, such as SHRM, ATD, HR Executive, HR Dive, Human Resources Today, and more. His books have been used and cited by some of the world's most prestigious universities as a method for instructing the next generation of human resources professionals.

Ben spends his days as the Chief Research Officer for Lighthouse Research & Advisory, a firm that examines and delivers groundbreaking insights on the HR technology market as well as workforce trends in hiring, training, retention, and more. He hosts the We're Only Human podcast, serves as chairperson for the HR Tech Awards, leads the HR Summer School series of events, and has written multiple books exploring human resources, technology, and the workplace.

When he's not spending time with his wife and children, he loves ice cream, movies about the end of the world, and running in a variety of outlandish races for fun.

CONTENTS

Preface

Anyone who knows me knows that I'm not a doomsayer. When others get louder about a trend, I typically retreat into the data to confirm, understand, and validate whatever the trend may be. That includes a host of things, from the ever-present conversation on how to "engage" our employees to conversations about "quiet quitting" and a host of other trendy buzzwords.

That's why the first section of this book (informally titled "Let's Commiserate Over How the Workforce is Shrinking") isn't the **whole book**. I'd rather be sure that each of you get some ideas to tackle the current and future challenges with hiring and retaining workers than spend tens of thousands of words to give you a really clear problem and no hope for what's next. Frankly, it's not my style. There are plenty of others out there that are happy to spend their time peddling hype instead of offering real solutions.

That said, every company is going to face some the very hard truths of what you will read in the coming pages. Many of you already have in the last few years. Others may have been insulated from some of the changes to a degree, but that protection is not permanent.

While this book, like much of my daily work, is centered on the United States, I have taken intentional steps to incorporate global data wherever possible to highlight similar challenges and problems in countries like India, China, Germany, and elsewhere. Make no mistake, this is a global issue, and while I'm contributing to the solution, this book isn't a cure-all for a landscape where talent scarcity is a reality.

Confession: I've been known to be a bit impatient at times. If you are the kind of person that likes to fast forward to the end of the movie to find out if the hero lives or skip to the end of the novel to see how things turn out, I get it. If you are more interested in some practical, innovative strategies and ideas about hiring and retention than in the causes of the tight labor market, feel free to jump to Section Two of the book. No judgment here.

If you'd like to see an incredible visual representation of the talent scarcity contributors and some of the potential solutions, I had my amazing designer whip up something special just for you. To get that resource and a video highlighting some of the stories of the innovative companies I'm watching closely, simply visit

TalentScarcity.com

1

WE ASKED 5,000 PEOPLE WHAT THEY NEED AT WORK: HERE'S WHAT WE FOUND (AND WHY IT MATTERS)

"The Great Resignation." It's been a term on everyone's lips in the last year and a half, and it's rapidly become a way for the world to talk about what's happening in the labor market with a catch-all term. But when speaking with business and talent leaders, it quickly becomes apparent that they have a unanimous perspective on this phrase: they **hate** it.

Sure, it may be catchy, but it paints a grim picture of these leaders standing on a beach with their feet rooted firmly to the ground. They can't move even a bit, and a tidal wave is coming in to crash over them as they stand helpless to prevent it. They can't run. They can't hide. They have to just stand there and watch it come for them. That's the sense many leaders (perhaps you, as well) have when it comes to this Great Resignation term, and it honestly feels hopeless. During a recent speech on this topic, an attendee specifically told me the term was "unhelpful," because it only pointed out an obvious problem and didn't indicate any sort of solution.

As a researcher and a bit of a skeptic at times, I told our team that we were going to do some digging on this to see if it was really true. Is the tidal wave coming for us with no way to avoid it, or is there something we could actually do to help mitigate the risk it presents?

Turns out that the picture painted by the news was not exactly correct. In that research of thousands of workers over the span of a year and a half, we found that a relatively high number of them were planning to quit a job or had already done so. But we also found that across the board there were calls for help and support that employers could answer to save and retain these people. In other words: **this is addressable, if we're willing to listen, adapt, and change to meet the needs of the modern worker.**

This book was written not just to talk about that research, although we will do so when the context demands it. Instead, it was written to address the bigger coming challenge. According to economists, demographers, and labor market experts, this "talent shortage" we've experienced recently is the tip of the iceberg. And unlike those individuals and organizations that thrive on ratings based on how much they can scare or anger you, I feel called to talk about the facts of the situation in a way that gives you hope for the future. See, this isn't the first time in history that there's been a shift in talent resulting in a shortage.

If we take a step back to Europe in the Middle Ages, we find an interesting parallel. After the bubonic plague pandemic swept through Europe, there were fewer workers available to complete the various jobs that needed done. As most monarchs were known to do, the king established rules that attempted to force people to do his will. In this case, anyone under age 60 had to work, and the ruling set limits on the wages they could demand. These increasingly strict rules backfired as workers demanded more rights and protections.[1]

As with present day, there are multiple paths ahead for anyone seeking a labor force. You could try to keep doing the same old things and see what results that offered (hint: turnover and ineffective hiring), or you could increase wages and other benefits to try to appeal to the workforce in more unique ways.

Can I let you peek behind the curtain for a moment? As this book was being written, I debated the title of talent shortage or talent scarcity.

The term "shortage" is used regularly in the business world to refer to talent, skills, and the like. For instance, Korn Ferry's research points to an $8.5 **trillion** talent shortage globally because there aren't enough skilled workers to fill the jobs that currently exist[2]. In fact, the firm has estimated that 85 million jobs could go unfilled in the next few years simply because there aren't enough people to take them.

In economics terms, a shortage happens when demand exceeds supply. The moment that happens, price goes up to help offset the limited amount that is available. In practical terms, it's just like when there are more home buyers in a market than the number of homes available, we call that a "seller's market" because sellers hold power in negotiations of a scarce resource and can command higher prices from buyers.

The good thing about those situations is that they normalize over time. More home builders enter the market to meet the high demand, and the prices begin to stabilize as demand and supply even out. However, what if those home builders didn't have enough raw materials? Or what if they didn't have any space to put new homes? Or what if they just stopped doing business in construction and opened flower shops, restaurants, and other types of companies instead? In that case we couldn't alleviate the pressure and prices would continue to skyrocket, necessitating a different set of options and alternatives to solve the problem.

That's when it becomes scarcity, which is worse. For comparison purposes, water is scarce in the desert. It's all but impossible to get it there in mass quantities, no matter how much demand there might be. Scarcity is defined as something being in short supply and is a naturally occurring limitation. As we get into Chapter two, you will see exactly why I call this "scarcity" and not just "shortage."

Scarcity is where the talent market is headed. Now, I want to be careful not to be alarmist or fearful. I want to present the facts as they exist today throughout this book so you can understand the micro and macroeconomic forces at play. It's unfair for me or anyone else to expect you to do your job well if you only have part of the information you'll need to be successful. At the same time, this isn't just going to written as a dark cloud of doom (although I've been told that sells a lot of books). After I share some of the realities that exist, I'll talk about various solutions that can enable us to mitigate them in some cases and potentially solve them in others. If you finish this book feeling helpless, hopeless, or defeated, then I've failed in my job. The future isn't without its challenges, true, but humanity has this excellent track record for stubbornly beating the odds.

One final note before we get to the book's content: while the economy ebbs and flows on the short-term, the concepts and ideas in this book are discussed with the long view in mind. Whether we end up in a recession or a booming economy over the next year or the next decade, the facts presented in this book are still the facts that we have to deal with sooner or later. This isn't a problem we can tackle easily, but that doesn't mean we shouldn't try to solve it anyway.

All that said, here's what you can expect in the coming pages:

Section One: Contributors to Talent Scarcity

Chapter two: Demographic Changes – this chapter will explore the various demographic changes that are happening both in North America and worldwide at a high level. This is one of the biggest drivers of the future talent shortage and we can't skip over the details here if we want to really grasp what is to come.

Chapter three: Personal Reprioritization and the Opportunity Cost of Work – the events of the last few years have shown, and our research has validated, that people are making different choices and setting different personal priorities. This will dive into some of those research findings as well as some interesting coverage of what's been called the "Antiwork" movement, plus some other personal choices that affect how many workers are available in the labor market.

Chapter four: Gigs, Entrepreneurs, and the Business Boom – this will explore how the entrepreneurial spirit is drawing people on a part-time and full-time basis from traditional employment and into a passion area, including data on new business growth and insights from our research on worker priorities. It also wraps in how employers can tap into this "entrepreneurial spirit" to attract and retain workers.

Section Two: Solutions to Talent Scarcity

Chapter five: Finding Workers in Innovative Ways – with a shallower talent pool, we'll need to be creative in how we attract people into our organizations. This isn't about hiring bonuses and free beer in the office fridge (though those don't hurt). It's about a more strategic look at what makes people tick and how to align with that, including case studies of organizations that are hiring in creative ways, such as Televerde, who operates call centers within multiple women's prisons worldwide, offering valuable work opportunities where others wouldn't think to go.

Chapter six: Employee Retention in the New Era – the retention of great workers has always been a priority of employers, but there's often been a mismatch on ownership, reporting, and action when it comes to employee turnover. We'll get into why that needs to change and some ways it can be improved. In addition, we'll cover the most common reasons workers leave jobs in the current market and how employers can address those critical issues.

Chapter seven: Technology and Automation as Gap Fillers – with fewer people to go around, we need to be making some decisions about where to embed technology, what problems it should solve, and how to make that leap without slowing the pace of business or creating an inhuman workplace for the workforce.

Chapter eight: Change, Agility, and Resetting Expectations – if we take all of the challenges above to be accurate, then what has to be true in order for businesses and leaders to succeed in such an environment? In the final chapter, we'll bring it all together and examine how talent issues are increasingly rising to the level of business issues and what it means for the future of work.

As mentioned before, the goal of this is not to give you concern or fear about the future. It's to give you some practical ideas, innovative strategies, and helpful solutions to face what's ahead instead of being blindsided unexpectedly. Ready? Let's go.

---

[1]   https://www.the-future-of-commerce.com/2021/08/30/history-repeats-pandemic-labor-shortage-great-resignation/

[2] https://www.kornferry.com/insights/this-week-in-leadership/talent-crunch-future-of-work

Section 1:
Contributors to Talent Scarcity

2

DEMOGRAPHIC CHANGES
AND IMPACTS

I'm probably average in a lot of things. In some areas, I'm definitely below average—just ask me sometime about the mishaps and mistakes I've had while attempting to construct, well, anything. Let's just say that I won't be asked to build any fine furniture anytime soon. However, in one area of life, I am most definitely above average. According to one source, the average number of children per family in the United States is about 1.9.[3] With four kids, my family is clearly an outlier, and our friends with five, six, or even more children are further outside the norm.

Why the kid discussion? Birth rates. But before I get to the young ones, let me talk about people at the other end of the spectrum: Baby Boomers.

At an event called "Diversity Promising Practices," hosted by Auburn University, I had the pleasure of seeing Professor James Johnson speak about the impact of demographic changes in the workplace. The key elements of his research focus on trends in demographics within the United States. If you're not based in the U.S., stay with me because I have some global numbers and evidence to show as well, and both sets of data are running pretty much in parallel.

The key trends in Johnson's research include elements like what he calls the "silver tsunami." To boil it down to the bare facts, the oldest Baby Boomers officially started reaching age 65 more than 10 years ago on January 1, 2011. From that point forward, between 8,000 to 10,000 Boomers reached that threshold **every day for the next 10-plus years**.

While time will tell what the lasting effects of the global COVID-19 pandemic will have on the workplace as a whole, one thing that we know for sure is that more people took that moment to retire than were expected to.[4] According to Pew Research, between 2008 and 2019, the retired population ages 55 and older grew by about 1 million retirees per year. In the past few years since the pandemic began, the ranks of retirees 55 and older have grown by 3.5 million.[5] For those of you that don't have a calculator handy, that's a 250% change in what was expected. While some of those retirees came back to the workforce in 2022 in the middle of the biggest talent shortage on record, there is a ticking clock on how long those workers can continue to contribute before they step back into retirement.[6]

This is playing out on a company-by-company level across the country, especially in organizations that tend to have populations of more experienced workers or those with abnormally high tenure. In a recent discussion with an HR leader from a global technology firm with 50,000 employees scattered across 50 different countries, this has been a reality their People team has had to grapple with in the last 24 months. The company has seen more people retire than expected and has had to adjust its retention and hiring plans accordingly. *At the end of chapter four, there's a helpful case study that highlights how one company is making this retiree population a strength instead of a weakness.*

The Birth Rate Problem

Now let's take this problem and make it more difficult, shall we? Remember the birth rate discussion that started this chapter? According to government statistics, the birth rate has been steadily declining over the last 15 years. When we add that to the fact that we're losing more senior and experienced workers than we're adding to the future workforce, it quickly becomes apparent that the tight labor market of the last year or two may get better in the short term, but much, much worse in the long term.

Remember, this isn't just a North American phenomenon. It's happening across the world, according to data from the Institute for Health Metrics and Evaluation at the University of Washington. As the graphic below indicates, this falloff, and the associated projections, are cause for concern.

Women are having fewer children

Global fertility rate (livebirths per woman)

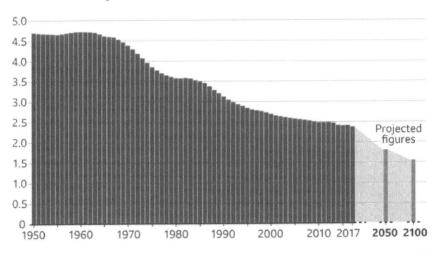

Source: Institute for Health Metrics and Evaluation at the University of Washington   BBC

Figure 2.1

We can go country by country and see these numbers playing out. According to the World Health Organization, the following birth rates (listed in livebirths per woman) exist across the world:

- China (1.28)
- United States (1.64)
- India (2.05)
- Germany (1.53)

- Russia (1.50)
- Mexico (1.90)
- Brazil (1.65)

The list goes on and on. I'm not a demographic scientist, but the replacement birth rate according to those researchers is 2.1, meaning each woman needs to have 2.1 children on average in order to maintain the existing population or it will begin to shrink. For comparison purposes, as evidenced in the previous chart, the birth rate in 1990 globally was right around 3.0 births per woman.

One country that's facing a particularly acute version of this issue is Japan (birth rate per woman is 1.34). There have been countless news stories and research efforts in recent years as Japan has tried to decide how to contend with its ballooning aging population (and subsequent shrinking population over time).[7] This affects everything from the labor market, as we are discussing within these pages but also things like economic policy (how do we pay out social security or retiree benefits when those individuals make up the majority of the population?), infrastructure (do we have enough caretakers and medical facilities to support the increased need for medical care in old age?), and so much more.[8] It is an incredibly difficult situation, and it's one that every country will face at some point if the birth rates globally continue to trend downward as they have over time.

While some companies are offering things like fertility benefits, most of the data on the actual adoption and/or usage rates comes from the companies that offer the benefits themselves, so there isn't yet any objective industry or academic data on how much they affect the workforce. Some may say that parental leave is another employer lever here that we can use to increase the birth rate, but that doesn't seem likely. Many countries around the world have mandatory parental leave protection, but those policies have not stemmed the dropping birth rate. Within the U.S., parental leave is not a federally mandated law, and data indicate that about 35% of companies offer maternity leave and 27% offer paternity leave.[9]

This isn't a book that is purely about demographics and global birth rates, but if this conversation is as intriguing to you as it is to me, there are amazing resources on this that go way deeper into this topic. If you want to know more, you can follow Professor James Johnson at the University of North Carolina or read books like *What to Expect When No One is Expecting* or *Empty Cradle*. These demographic challenges and changes are bigger than the workplace, and the solutions to them will have to come from outside the workplace as well.

Challenges of an Aging Workforce

For any society that requires younger workers to pay into a system that benefits retirees, this conversation is a real issue. Like with the Japanese example above, at some point the number of people collecting benefits outnumbers the number of people paying in to create those benefits, which overburdens the system. If we have fewer people around to do the work, that's one problem. But another issue that immediately becomes obvious is the lack of experienced workers to train, educate, and apprentice those younger workers entering into new disciplines.

Some companies are working on ways to capture, transfer, and retain knowledge among the workforce, including the intriguing story in the case study later in this chapter. However, others aren't treating this issue with the level of respect it deserves. In our 2022 Learning Trends study, we found that two-thirds of talent leaders are worried about this knowledge leaving their workplace as people quit or retire. A few key problem areas emerge from this scenario:

1. **Decreased innovation**: the people take their ideas with them when they leave

2. **Less capacity for growth**: those that depart reduce the company's ability to grow consistently

3. **Less efficiency/increased costs**: the staff that replace those who left are less capable, at least initially, and require training to get up to speed

4. **Loss of competitive advantage**: the workforce/people are often cited as the competitive advantage for most companies—losing any key players truly can be a loss of a key differentiator

If experienced leaders with a strategic perspective of how the organization operates end up leaving, they take their brains along with them. That knowledge and innovation may not have a measurable cost the day they leave, but over the long term it will be incredibly costly. A parallel to this concept that makes it easier to understand is the shift to remote work in recent years.

Research shows that one of the indirect costs of remote work is a reduction in what I call "casual innovation" at work.[10] In an office environment, if Melissa has an idea, she can grab Miguel and Sharice for a quick brainstorming session. That type of casual, spontaneous innovation doesn't happen as often in a virtual or remote environment, because we need to ask for time on someone's calendar to get together, we don't have the visual cues of seeing other brainstorming partners, and other barriers. Many times, we don't even bring it up because it feels like the threshold for having a conversation is too high, especially if the outcomes are unclear as they typically are in a brainstorming session. However, we don't have as many reservations with doing that in person (how many of us have had meetings that could have been handled with a single, brief email?) This reduction in casual innovation doesn't have a visible/tangible cost on day one of remote work, but over the course of time it becomes a sort of negative compounding return due to the loss of ideas shared, explored, and implemented.

That negative cost is similar in many respects to the cost of losing senior, experienced workers. We may not count the cost of losing that person the day they leave, the next day, or even the next month, but over the course of time, that price will absolutely be paid.

Bottom line: the demographic element to this bigger challenge is one that we can't ignore. Companies can try to address it today, and they absolutely should, but over time these demographic shifts may become increasingly frenetic as the pool of talent continues to shrink.

Workforce Depletion Model
Approximate labor force: 165 million workers
Estimated 1.75 million retirees per year based on recent findings[11]
Running Total Depletion: 1.75 million workers
Possible to retain: yes
Willing/able to return to work: yes, at least temporarily

What is this Workforce Depletion Model? As we proceed through the contributors to talent scarcity, you will see a running calculation of the number of people who could be leaving the workforce and whether that group of workers can or can't be retained or hired back. This is to provide a rough idea of how large these impacts are to the workforce on a cumulative basis.

Case Study: Tackling Knowledge Transfer from Experienced to Junior Workers

One company we worked with a few years ago had an intriguing approach to the challenge of knowledge transfer at work. The manufacturer's average employee tenure was unusually high, with most employees staying there for 20 years, and some even had 30 years of service at the high end. In other words, a new hire remained the "new person" on the team until they had been at the company for at least seven or eight years. That feeling of being on the outside created the only real turnover the company faced, which was within someone's first year on the job.

With this pressure on the new hires to feel like part of the team, the company's leaders began looking for ways to develop deeper connections among the workforce and close the gap between the new and existing staff. In the end, the organization created its Senior Professionals Onboarding Training program, or SPOT for short. Put simply, it paired new hires with a more experienced worker to learn the ropes of the technology, tools, and processes. Perhaps more importantly, at least from a retention aspect, these relationships also brought forth the cultural norms and values of the organization. Our research shows that one of the top things new hires want when they take a job isn't just to know the tasks they need to accomplish but to be connected to their peers and the values of the organization.[12] In that regard, this program was designed to meet those specific needs.

Incidentally, the company also realized an unexpected benefit from this arrangement. Many of those workers with long tenure were capped out in their pay rates and were only eligible to receive cost of living increases, and the company didn't have many opportunities to increase their compensation or modify their responsibilities. The SPOT program gave them a chance to incentivize those workers with meaningful mentoring opportunities and public recognition of their contributions without breaking the budget. While there was some initial hesitation about how the program might be received by these experienced workers, it became clear that the opportunity to be a SPOT mentor was a choice opportunity to contribute to the success of a teammate and the organization in a profound way.

Ultimately, the program had the double benefit of creating stronger ties for the new hires and also helping those more experienced workers to be able to mentor others, paying forward their expertise in the field and giving them a new and valuable way to support the business and their new peers.

---

[3] https://www.statista.com/statistics/718084/average-number-of-own-children-per-family/

[4] https://www.kansascityfed.org/research/economic-bulletin/what-has-driven-the-recent-increase-in-retirements/

[5] https://www.pewresearch.org/fact-tank/2021/11/04/amid-the-pandemic-a-rising-share-of-older-u-s-adults-are-now-retired/

[6] https://www.washingtonpost.com/business/2022/05/05/retirement-jobs-work-inflation-medicare/

[7] https://www.imf.org/external/pubs/ft/fandd/2001/03/muhleise.htm

[8] https://www.oecd-ilibrary.org/sites/8f7fecd9-en/index.html?itemId=/content/component/8f7fecd9-en

[9] https://www.hrdive.com/news/shrm-parental-leave-findings-decreased-benefits-offerings/632958

[10] https://www.nature.com/articles/s41562-021-01196-4

[11] https://www.stlouisfed.org/on-the-economy/2022/january/great-retirement-who-are-retirees

[12] https://lhra.io/blog/more-tech-more-headcount-more-budget-early-findings-from-our-new-talent-acquisition-research/

3

PERSONAL REPRIORITIZATION
AND THE OPPORTUNITY COST OF WORK

I still remember one of the most beautiful, spiritual moments I have experienced as a runner. It was 2:14 in the morning. I was on a dark Kentucky road with my headlight bobbing in the darkness. I couldn't see another person or vehicle, so I shut off my headlight to run under the full moon for just a few minutes. It was pure bliss.

This brief moment happened in the middle of what was a pretty hectic 48 hours as my team and I raced in the Bourbon Chase, a 200-mile relay across the state of Kentucky with major transition points at the well-known bourbon distilleries like Wild Turkey, Maker's Mark, and Four Roses. Life was busy with work, small children at home, volunteering, and other responsibilities, but I had made the decision to prioritize running that event with friends, so I did.

Lots of people make that same decision to prioritize or reprioritize themselves, their families, and other personal needs every day. When our fourth child was born, my wife Melanie decided she wanted to stay home with her. She had returned to work after the births of our first three kids, but this one seemed different to her somehow because it was our last planned child. That moment reshuffled her personal and professional priorities for the first time in 10 years of working as a highly capable elementary school teacher. The decision came with no small amount of guilt and worry about what others might think, but our family decision was to support whatever she felt was best for her.

Her decision at the most fundamental level is what so many people in the workforce have done in the last few years. They are making different decisions about what their priorities are, and we have seen in our research that many business leaders are shocked that those priorities often didn't include working for their company, resulting in employee turnover.

Those different decisions can have a spectrum of variables. For example:

- I don't want to work for *this kind* of company
- I don't want to work in *this kind* of job
- I don't want to work for *this kind* of leader
- It's more important for me to spend time with my kids or other family members now
- It's more important for me to control my own destiny as an entrepreneur or gig worker

Remember the discussion about The Great Resignation earlier in the book and how business leaders hate the term? The research study we did to examine the phenomenon actually found something incredible: workers were telling us that instead of it just being about a mass wave of resignations, many of the decisions were instead driven by personal reprioritization.

Special thanks to ChenMed Chief Learning Officer Christopher Lind for coining the term "The Great Reprioritization," because that's exactly what the data points indicate.

There's a term in economics called "opportunity cost." It simply means that every decision we make has a cost to it, even if that cost is simply what we missed out on. As an example, if I want to eat lunch with friends, the opportunity cost might be finishing that report I'm writing or having lunch with my kids. In work terms, the opportunity cost of work drives some of this reprioritization shift. People decide that the time away from family or the time deprioritizing their personal needs is no longer satisfactory, which pushes them to choose a different path.

When I worked as an HR executive, this happened in one of our facilities. Mac was a team leader supporting clients at a government facility. He did great work, maintained an excellent relationship with the customer, and was well loved by his team. Yet one day he turned in his resignation. Upon investigating, I found that Mac was satisfied with his work, but he no longer needed to work for financial reasons. In the end, he just wanted more time with his grandchildren and to spend on fishing and personal pursuits.

For most companies, that would have been the end of Mac's employment. However, I wanted to try something unique, so I asked Mac if he would be interested in working two days a week of his own choosing and spending the rest of the time on his own personal priorities. Mac was stunned at the option, because he never even considered that something like that would be possible. Over the next 18 months, Mac had the opportunity to work at his own pace and continue contributing his valuable mentorship and ideas. At the same time, the company was able to bring in a new team leader under Mac's guidance while maintaining a critical customer relationship during the transition.

This exchange cost virtually nothing, since both of these workers were supporting a client project with billable hours, and it netted many hours of honorable, consistent service from a trusted team member. I learned something valuable through this experience: employers that look at flexibility on an individual level will take on more work, but the payoff in dedication and performance nearly always outweighs any associated cost.

For many, the 2020 pandemic created a moment to pause and reflect on what mattered most. In a 2011 book written by Bronnie Ware, she explored the top regrets of the dying based on her experiences as a caregiver.[13] When we look at those, we can see exactly why people stepped back from work and stepped toward personal connection and/or reconnection. A few of those regrets:

1. I wish I'd lived a life true to myself, not the life others expected of me
2. I wish I hadn't worked so much

3. I wish I'd stayed in touch with friends

These kinds of regrets can create powerful, actionable emotions that drive us to different types of decisions. However, in some cases, the shift around priorities was even stronger, with some workers deciding that they didn't want to work at all.

Personal and Family Prioritization: The Opportunity Cost of Work

I began this chapter with the personal story of my wife's decision to come home with our kids, but I'll continue it now. While I we can't say what the future holds, she's back to work part time now that all of our kids have reached school age.

This kind of personal decision is one that isn't permanent, but we saw a tremendous amount of it in 2020 and 2021 as women stepped away from the workforce. Whether by intentional choice or by default due to circumstances, millions of women left the workforce in one fell swoop.[14] Key reasons for this included everything from burnout and stress (top reasons in our data for job departures in 2021) to a lack of childcare options to support full time work.

Thousands of childcare facilities closed during COVID, and some of them were never able to restart operations due to a shortage of staff or other limitations. I served on a board of directors for a childcare facility during the pandemic, and it was heartbreaking to see the difficulty it placed on families during the times the facility could not operate.

Some new 2022 data show that while many women stepped back from the workplace during 2020, about half of them returned to work by 2021 and the other half by 2022. Over that two-year period, women have begun refilling roles they left during the pandemic, due in part to some of the drivers we are all familiar with:

- rising costs,
- easing COVID restrictions,
- and a return to in-person school for children.

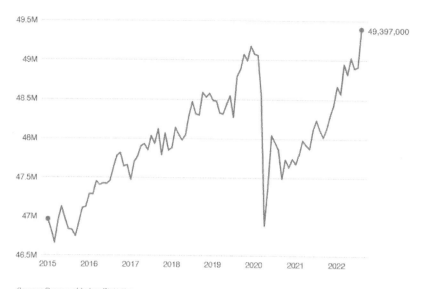

Source: Bureau of Labor Statistics
Credit: Connie Hanzhang Jin and Scott Horsley/NPR

Figure 3.1[15]

While we will dive into practical solutions for targeting women and bringing them back into the workplace in later chapters, I'd like to quickly highlight one organization that tackled this challenge head-on. During the early days of the pandemic, I spoke with Donielle Buie from the Broad Institute of MIT and Harvard. She explained how the Institute was supporting its staff with emergency childcare coverage to help them continue working and maintaining some semblance of normalcy in a world that was anything but normal.[16] The story was a powerful one and highly relevant at the time, because the Broad Institute does biological and chemical research, both of which were incredibly important during the early days of the pandemic as everyone searched for solutions to a global problem.

Parents have always had a pull on them. In some professions with a high percentage of women (education, nursing, etc.), it is expected that some of the workforce will be out of work on maternity leave at any one time. And a portion of those workers are likely to change their mind about returning to work once they have had time to settle in and bond with a child. It's not right or wrong, it's just a reality.

Some parents and families have the flexibility for someone to stay home with children, and others don't. One of our great friends has multiple children and homeschools them all, which is a wonderful setup for their family, but it wouldn't work for ours. The thing that employers have to see, and we'll highlight this more in case studies of Audible and an aerospace research firm later in the book, is that a paycheck isn't always enough to get someone to change their entire family structure. There needs to be something else. Making a choice to return to work for some people feels like they are betraying or giving up on their most important family responsibilities, and it can seem like a no-win situation.

I recently heard about a manufacturing firm that was struggling to find enough workers. They kept hearing from applicants that they needed flexibility and couldn't accept the job's hours from 7:00am to 4:00pm daily due to childcare responsibilities. After hearing that same reason multiple times, the company decided to pilot a "parent shift" with work hours between 8:30am and 2:00pm to accommodate the bulk of the requests. The results were unexpected.

Not only did the company get a number of people to accept the job, but productivity rates during the **shorter** parent shift were better than those during the longer standard shift employees. In a five-and-a-half-hour workday, these workers were accomplishing more than those people working a standard eight-hour day.

Why? I haven't had the benefit of talking with those employees directly, but if I did, I imagine that I'd hear things like:

- Someone **finally gave me a chance** to show what I can do.
- I'm so **thankful for the opportunity to contribute**.
- Now I **don't have to choose** between work and my family.

We'll explore the idea of flexible work schedules more fully as a retention strategy later, but this is a great example of how they can meet the needs of the business and the needs of the workforce at the same time.

Because we see in the data that women have returned to the workforce in full strength from the COVID dip, I'm not adding the number of those impacted into the Workforce Depletion Model.

What's a NILF? The Missing Link

When I picture a world of talent scarcity, pretty much every person who is willing to work has an opportunity to do so. But there's a concerning number of people who are missing from the labor force and demographers and economists aren't sure why. Called "not in the labor force," or NILF for short, these individuals are by every standard able to work but aren't pursuing it.[17]

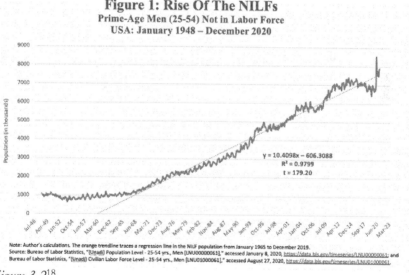

Figure 1: Rise Of The NILFs
Prime-Age Men (25-54) Not in Labor Force
USA: January 1948 – December 2020

$$y = 10.4098x - 606.3088$$
$$R^2 = 0.9799$$
$$t = 179.20$$

Note: Author's calculations. The orange trendline traces a regression line in the NILF population from January 1965 to December 2019.
Source: Bureau of Labor Statistics, "(Unadj) Population Level - 25-54 yrs., Men [LNU00000061]," accessed January 8, 2020, https://data.bls.gov/timeseries/LNU00000061; and Bureau of Labor Statistics, "(Unadj) Civilian Labor Force Level - 25-54 yrs., Men [LNU01000061]," accessed August 27, 2020, https://data.bls.gov/timeseries/LNU01000061.

Figure 3.2[18]

The drivers on why this phenomenon exists are mixed:

- In 2021, at least 45% of NILF men and women without kid reported taking pain medication each day.
- Time use studies among these demographics show an alarming amount of daily screen time (4-6 hours a day).[19]
- Data indicate that these individuals are spending more

time on leisure activities than any other group.

I'm not sure I have the answers to solve a problem both as large and long-standing as this, but it's relevant to this bigger picture conversation.

Workforce Depletion Model
Approximate labor force: 165 million workers
Estimated 7 million civilian, non-institutionalized men between the ages of 25 and 54[20]
Running Total Depletion: 8.75 million workers
Possible to retain: uncertain
Willing/able to return to work: uncertain

The Antiwork Movement

Kids these days.

That phrase has been used since the beginning of time to explain away the changing social expectations and perceptions of the next generation. One of my favorite examples comes from a 1920 article that says, "No longer is it true that the young are seen but not heard. Not only do they make themselves heard, but they shout down their elders in a daily mounting chorus... Art, literature, education, and economics—all are being dominated more and more by the reckless, half-formed judgments of youth."

One of those judgments in modern times is what's been called the Antiwork movement. What is the Antiwork movement? There are a few components, but the key focus is that these individuals believe that they should work "just enough" and no additional hours to "create excess capital or goods." In recent history, this type of working to a limited standard has also been associated with the "quiet quitting" phenomenon. One portrayal of this phenomenon is workers who do just enough work to keep their job but nothing more.

While time will tell how or if this Antiwork concept will catch on more broadly or if it will fizzle out, it currently only seems to reflect the views of a small minority of workers. Most importantly, it signifies a bigger trend: **workers are skeptical of employers more than ever, and the unfulfilled promises and workplace turmoil of recent years has jaded more workers than we'd like to admit.**

As an example, we found in our hiring research that eight out of 10 candidates want to hear about career advancement opportunities during the hiring process.[21] That's much more than expected, and in direct follow-ups with respondents we discovered that it's due in part to broken promises. In the past, workers would ask about career opportunities and the hiring manager would promise to revisit the discussion after the worker's first review, after a probationary period, etc. However, those individuals found that once they accepted the job, they lost their leverage. In many cases, could never force that conversation to happen again. In a market where candidates are juggling multiple offers, they have the leverage to force that conversation to happen earlier in the hiring process so they can more comprehensively compare and contrast the jobs available to them.

If we juxtapose this storyline with the incredible Nussbaum employee retention case study at the end of Chapter Six, something occurs to me: this conversation may be less about antiwork and more about being anti-companies-and-managers-that-don't-care-about-people. The root of this dislike, mistrust, or general unpleasant feelings about work isn't coming from people who love their work, feel supported by a great manager, and have a company that supports them not just as an employee but as a **human being**.

Let's get personal here for a moment. I don't always remember the times I accepted a new job, but I can remember nearly every time I decided to leave. Do you remember a time when you decided to leave a job for another one? I do. I was sitting at a celebratory dinner after the completion of a major project, feeling very good about what had been accomplished by the team in such a short time. My boss came and sat next to me, looked me in the eye, and said, "I just want you to remember, nobody really cares what you say. They only care about you because you work for me." That conversation may have happened years ago, but I still feel the surprise and pain that came with it as I tell the story right here and now. I'm happy to say that both of those emotions were immediately offset, though, by the **instant resolve** I felt to find a new role where my hard work would be appreciated and valued. I wouldn't put up with that kind of abuse any longer. All of us would like to think that those kinds of managers only exist in wacky movies and television shows for their comedic value, but they are very real. These people are major contributors to workers feeling like **work is broken**, even though it only means their **primary relationship at work** is broken.

I'll close this discussion on antiwork with this: after the second edition of my book *Artificial Intelligence for HR: Use AI to support and develop a successful workforce* was released, I received a note on LinkedIn from an engineer in Europe who had read the book. His first comment? *I don't understand.*

But when I read further, I found that as an engineer, he understood the technical aspects of AI technology perfectly. The part he struggled with was where I wrote about the employers that supported the members of their employee population with tools, resources, and a caring culture. See, in his 20+ years of work experience, he told me that he'd never worked for an employer that cared about him like these companies I was writing about. It might as well have been a fictional book based on his own work experiences.

This is one of the reasons I do this kind of work every day, educating talent and business leaders just like you with books, speaking, and other resources. It's not just for us, but it's for workers like that who need to know that their work has meaning, their skills have value, and that we don't take that for granted.

Drug Overdose Deaths

I'll start off by admitting that drug overdose is stretched a bit to be included in a section about personal choices, because people often don't have much choice if they become addicted to pain medications or have a predisposition towards illicit substances due to life situation or genetics. Whatever those drivers may be, it's a real problem.

According to the Centers for Disease Control, nearly 70,000 people died in the US in 2020 alone from opioid overdose deaths. When we expand that to any drug-involved overdose, the number of deaths climbs to nearly 92,000.

The trendlines on each of these graphs is upward, meaning more people die every year than the year before. Provisional data puts these deaths at 100,000+ if we use a 12-month period ending on January 2022. Purely from an economical vantage point, that's 100,000+ people who can't fill a role, complete a task, or hold a job. On a global level, it's estimated that just under 1% of all workers are dependent or addicted to a form of illegal drugs, with some countries having higher dependent populations and some lower.[22] That's more than 30 million people when we consider it in the context of a global workforce of three billion people. The New York Post even shone a spotlight on this issue, highlighting the fact that more than 70,000 truck drivers failed drug tests and were removed from duty, further exacerbating an industry that has claimed a shortage of workers for decades.[23]

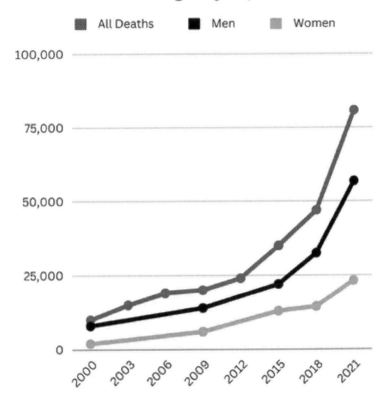

Figure 3.3[24]

Source: Centers for Disease Control and
Prevention, National Center for Health Statistics

While it's a fraction of the overall global workforce, this is still a contributor to the overall talent shortage, and when factored with some of these other elements we're covering in this book, you realize that while it may sound a bit cliched, **every single person counts**. Every life matters. Unlike a personal choice to stay home with children or a decision to retire early, every drug overdose death is a permanent impact on society, communities, families, and yes, the workplace.

By the way, researchers have to ask hard, uncomfortable questions sometimes. And one of those is this: you might assume that these drug-dependent individuals may not be working anyway, so what impact does this really have on the number of available workers? The truth is nearly two out of three workers using illicit drugs are in full-time jobs, according to one 2016 study.[25] These are our employees, neighbors, friends, and coworkers, even if we may not realize the challenges they are facing.

From an employer perspective, offering substance abuse support could be a practical, tangible way to help alleviate this issue to some degree. With more companies leaning into mental health and wellbeing benefits, this type of support might be valuable to consider adding, though our research shows that substance abuse is offered less often than other types of health and wellbeing resources.[26]

Additionally, if we can target those professions where opioid deaths are prevalent, we might have a more measurable impact on saving lives. The same 2016 CDC study highlighted some key job categories where the number of opioid deaths were higher than expected, which may offer a sort of ranked list of priorities if your organization operates in the following industries:

1. Mining
2. Construction
3. Health care practitioners
4. Health care support
5. Personal care and services
6. Food preparation and serving

Bottom line: it's a serious issue, and even if it may be classified as a social problem, it's impacting employers, families, **and** society by removing people from the workforce and from our communities. Each and every one of us is more than just a job. If you or someone you know is facing these challenges, please contact a free hotline within your specific country to get help.

Workforce Depletion Model
Approximate labor force: 165 million workers
Estimated 107,000 annual deaths based on CDC figures[27]
Running Total Depletion: 8.751 million workers
Possible to retain: only via early interventions to save lives
Willing/able to return to work: no

Case Study: Casual Retirement Program Boosts Talent Available to $900M Aerospace Organization

When people retire from a job, they typically leave the workforce and move on with their lives. However, that's not the case at Aerospace Corp. This global engineering company realized that it had a fairly large number of employees retiring and returning to work as consultants and contractors immediately thereafter. To create a more seamless process and increase participation, Aerospace leadership instituted the "retiree casual" program which allows former employees to join a pool of available workers for hire. Each individual is limited to 1,000 hours a year (an average of 19-20 hours a week, if they want to work that much).[28]

These individuals can do special projects, solve problems, or fill other gaps on a short-term basis as needed. The company has about 250 retirees actively participate in the program each year, which is extremely high when you consider the firm's full employee headcount is below 4,000 staff. Leaders at Aerospace say that approximately 80% of retirees sign up for the program, and some of them return to work the day after their official retirement! Participants in the program cite a range of benefits:

- A chance to phase into retirement instead of an abrupt transition overnight
- Work that is meaningful and keeps them current in their skills
- Opportunities to spend more time on personal pursuits and interests, from family to hobbies and more
- Mentoring relationships with younger workers where they can pass on institutional knowledge

Long-term employees of the company can retire at age 55 with full medical benefits for life, but workers continue in this retiree program into their mid-sixties, and some continue to work beyond age 80. Work hours vary by person and by project, but some work a few days a week throughout the year while others work six months on and six months off to stay under the 1,000-hour limit. Unlike many companies that might have to hire expensive consultants to step into the gap, Aerospace can re-hire its existing workforce that already knows the customer, project structure, and other variables, gaining a flexible and highly qualified workforce that's available on demand.

13 https://www.theguardian.com/lifeandstyle/2012/feb/01/top-five-regrets-of-the-dying
14 https://www.uschamber.com/workforce/data-deep-dive-a-decline-of-women-in-the-workforce
15 https://www.npr.org/2022/09/28/1125149612/women-are-returning-to-paid-work-after-the-pandemic-forced-many-to-leave-their-j
16 https://blog.shrm.org/blog/handling-the-clash-of-parenting-and-work-in-a-pandemic
17 https://nypost.com/2022/11/02/disturbing-rise-of-the-nilfs-men-not-in-the-labor-force/
18 https://ifstudies.org/blog/what-do-prime-age-nilf-men-do-all-day-a-cautionary-on-universal-basic-income
19 https://www.psychnewsdaily.com/average-screen-time-now-6-hours-per-day/
20 https://ifstudies.org/blog/what-do-prime-age-nilf-men-do-all-day-a-cautionary-on-universal-basic-income
21 https://lhra.io/blog/3-reasons-candidates-ghost-employers-plus-4-things-they-desire-infographic/
22 https://ourworldindata.org/illicit-drug-use?insight=just-under-1-of-the-world-has-an-illicit-drug-dependency#key-insights-on-illicit-drug-use
23 https://nypost.com/2021/11/07/supply-chain-stalled-by-72000-truckers-who-failed-drug-tests/
24 https://nida.nih.gov/research-topics/trends-statistics/overdose-death-rates
25 https://www.cdc.gov/mmwr/volumes/67/wr/pdfs/mm6733a3-H.pdf
26 https://lhra.io/blog/new-research-employees-score-companies-with-a-failing-grade-on-mental-health-support/
27
https://www.cdc.gov/nchs/pressroom/nchs_press_releases/2022/202205.htm
28 https://www.nytimes.com/2003/03/18/jobs/comebacks-retired-but-still-on-the-job.html

4

GIGS, ENTREPRENEURS, AND THE BUSINESS BOOM

One of the biggest and most intriguing studies into the gig economy in 2015 showed massive growth in the number of people who were doing gig work across the United States. The data indicated a whopping 50% growth in the number of gig workers, signifying a massive shift in the workforce. The findings served as an indicator that the economy was going to become more reliant on gig and contingent work, and it supported everyone's perceptions of Uber and other similar companies that were offering flexible work options for those that wanted them. Everything was changing, and we all had a front row seat to the evolution of work as we knew it.

Too bad the study was wrong.

Recently, the authors of the study have come out publicly to highlight why their findings were flawed and what actually occurred, and it seems that all the noise about everyone becoming a freelancer or contingent worker was pretty overblown. I'll say that again: **in spite of the loud proclamations that gig work is going to take over the world in recent years, the evidence shows that it's still a** relatively small portion of the overall workforce.[29] For instance, Intuit's 2017 predictions that 43% of the U.S. workforce would be gig workers by 2020 was definitely incorrect, but we have to consider the source.[30] Intuit's accounting products are used by companies of varying sizes, and if a person sets up as a roofing contractor, ballet instructor, or keynote speaker in their free time, they technically show up as a gig worker, **even if every single one of those people is working a full-time or part-time day job.**

That said, consider this fact: if we merged all of the millions of global independent workers that drive for Uber into a single company as employees, that firm would be the largest employer on the planet, bigger than Amazon, McDonald's, or even Wal-Mart. Gig workers, or independent workers, are a major part of how work gets done today, whether it's their only source of income or a side hustle for someone in addition to their primary occupation. Data from Pew Research shows that as of 2021, 16% of Americans had earned money from an online gig platform.[31]

In a mini research project developed for a speech on changes in the gig economy and what that meant for employers, I had come across some intriguing findings from Princeton University and other sources on how people were picking up more freelance, contract, and independent work.[32] What amazed me, though, was a finding at the time that indicated an increase in W-9 income while W-2 roles remained fairly steady. To rephrase that: income from work that was not done for an employer (gigs, side jobs, contract work, etc.) increased **while people remained employed** at their jobs typically. This wasn't a wholesale change from traditional employment to gig work—it was the addition of what many affectionately call their "side hustle" to their primary income stream from a day job.

One can guess at some of the common reasons for that, including increased income to support personal finance decisions. Another is a desire to have work that feeds some part of them that they don't get at work. In a discussion with a Lyft driver in Chicago last year during a ride, she told me that she was a social worker by day. While she believed her work was meaningful, it left her drained emotionally after most of her shifts were complete. She loved to talk and used her Lyft time to laugh, connect, and serve others without having any of the emotional baggage of her day job following her home.

In that conversation and others, I found that the theme of flexibility kept recurring over and over again. If they were delivering food, driving people, or doing other on-demand work, they liked being able to turn it on or turn it off depending on their mood, available time, and need for extra income. Instead of fitting their life around their work, as is the case with many workers in full-time jobs, they were fitting their work around their life. That includes those doing it as a part-time activity and those that were full-time as well across dozens of interactions. In fact, Uber actually partnered with an external research firm to figure out why people drive with them, and the response for eight out of 10 drivers was flexibility (and a significant majority of them also wanted to be their own boss, not be bossed around by others).[33] I've personally heard that reasoning dozens of times with drivers for Uber, Lyft, and Gett (when traveling to London) over the years.

In one recent study of frontline workers specifically, we discovered that about 7% of them quit jobs in the last year to pursue contract or gig work on their own schedule. While that's not a massive percentage, imagine a restaurant with 30 staff. 7% of that workforce would be approximately two people, and if every restaurant in town lost two people, they would be forced to slow down service, limit the number of guests, and begin competing more heavily for talent in their local area. I can't speak for you, but that sounds incredibly familiar based on my own family's dining experiences in the last 12-18 months.

At a grander scale, McKinsey data indicate that the number of frontline workers totals approximately 112 million people in the U.S. alone.[34] If we net out 7% of those workers, that equals 7.8 million individuals who quit to pursue their own "thing" as a contractor, freelancer, or gig worker.

For what it's worth, there are many who think that gig work has a detrimental effect on workers and society. The U.S. Labor Secretary went so far as to claim in 2021 that most gig workers should be reclassified as employees.[35] Gig workers often have no access to benefits, healthcare, or other protections afforded normal employees. There have been attempts to rein in gig platforms and add protections for workers, but they have not been consistent. While it's too early to say what will ultimately change in this area, it's likely that we will see more standardized protections for this segment of the labor force as it continues to increase in size.

The Business Boom

Let's set aside the gig work conversation for a second and look at another data source: business startups. In our Great Reprioritization study, we saw an astounding one in three workers who quit their jobs in 2021 say that they started their own business.[36] While we didn't go deeper into this to understand more about the reasons or what those businesses look like, the data I'll share next help to validate these findings.

The government tracks data on companies starting up for the first time, and when we evaluate that in the context of the events of the last few years, the findings are shocking.

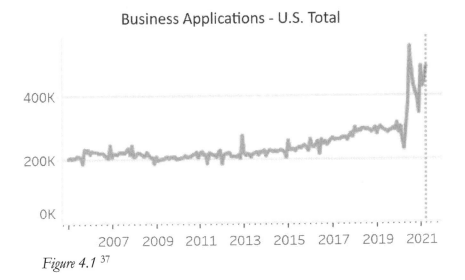

Figure 4.1 [37]

Beyond the dip when COVID hit in 2020 and shook up the economy, work, and our personal lives, **every month after that has seen a record number of business applications** compared to historical levels.

As for why, the reasons in some ways are the very same as those outlined previously: people want more financial stability, they want flexibility, and they want an outlet to do work that fills a specific need they have. If that requires them to leave a job and find a new one, so be it. But it can also entice them to step out of the traditional labor force and into their own business as well.

If you work for a large company, this discussion around small business may seem foreign to you, but it's bigger than you might imagine. Consider this data point: when you look at the 6.1 million employers in the United States, firms with 10 employees or less accounted for 78.5% of all businesses and firms with 500 or fewer employees accounted for 99.7% of all businesses.[38] Just 0.3% of firms (~18,000) in the U.S. have more than 500 employees, even though the firms in this group are the ones that are typically featured in the headlines as if they embody the majority of employers. Small businesses employ about half of all U.S. workers. This same breakdown occurs globally as well. For instance, 40% of India's labor force is employed by small enterprises.[39] In the UK, 99.5% of businesses have fewer than 50 employees.[40]

This concept of entrepreneurialism has its roots in those key needs that someone wants to fill. In other management theory we've seen that people crave autonomy (control), mastery (progress), and purpose (clear mission), and the entrepreneurial journey gives people that walk that path the opportunity to experience every one of those. We'll come back to this in the chapter on employee retention because the people who want to scratch that itch might be able to do so within your own company's walls if you're willing to give them a shot. The case study at the end of this chapter provides a great example of how Coca Cola did this internally.

From a practical perspective, more entrepreneurs and business startups equal fewer independent workers available to be employed full time. While the data points on how business startups intersect with the labor force aren't clear due to how the information is collected by the government, the information we do have is pretty compelling.

Consider the following statistics from the U.S. Census Bureau that relate to new business formation:

- Nearly 5.4 million applications were filed to form new businesses in 2021, the most of any year on record
- Those numbers represent a whopping 53% increase from 2019 applications[41]
- About one-third, or 1.8 million applications, were for likely employer businesses, which is a segment of applications that indicate the new businesses are likely to hire employees[42]

Not only that, but our own research showed that one-third of job quitters in Q4 of 2021 said they left their jobs to start their own companies. We don't know if those were solo shops or if they planned to hire workers, but the Census data above give us some idea that one out of three were for companies that would be likely to eventually hire staff.

Consider this a complicating factor when it comes to potential workers you can hire. **Not only is each of these people leaving the workforce, but they are starting companies that will eventually compete with you for workers.**

Note that this doesn't even take into account those individuals that are doing gig or contract work. While some of those workers are likely captured by the business formation statistics if they file for an employer identification number, many of them operate as independent contractors. For instance, rideshare drivers do not need to file for an employer identification number (EIN), but they can if they plan to file taxes as an entity other than a sole proprietor.

In the end, this is one of those contributors to talent scarcity that could be impermanent. Economic ebbs and flows, personal life changes, legislation, and other factors can shift how, when, and why people look to self-employment or gig work. Kapost, a company acquired by Upland Software in 2019, realized a number of its former employees were leaving to start their own companies. Instead of trying to figure out how to trap them or use golden handcuffs, the company began positioning its recruitment messaging to appeal to those individuals by highlighting its alumni that left the company to successfully begin their own firms. Think about the intellectual capital developed and grown by the company by bringing in those future startup founders and leveraging their insights and expertise during their tenure.

Employers that can tap into the internal creativity of the workforce can reap the benefits of a motivated group of high performers. While entrepreneurs are seen as "lone wolves," the truth is they are great at finding and solving problems, prioritizing activities that drive customer value, and managing within budgets and timelines. If asked, all of us would likely add those types of skills to our list of "wants" when it comes to the workers we hire.

Workforce Depletion Model
Approximate labor force: 165 million workers
Estimated 7% of workers based on recent survey[43]
Running Total Depletion: 20.3 million workers
Possible to retain: yes, at least partially
Willing/able to return to work: potentially

Talent Scarcity
Workforce Depletion Model
165 million Total U.S.
Labor Force

20.3 million workers
affected by the factors
below

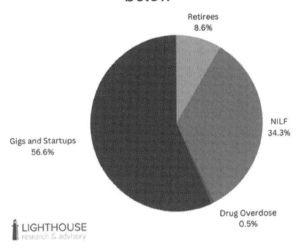

Figure 4.2

Notes: This model is for illustration purposes only. Some figures (retirement, overdose) are annual figures while NILF and gig/business startup figures are more of a snapshot in time of an ongoing trend that can rise/fall over time.

Case Study: Leveraging the Internal Entrepreneurial Spirit for New Innovation

When we think about innovation, we expect it to come from the technology industry or a new, cutting-edge firm. But what about a 130-plus year old company?

Coca-Cola is a globally recognized name, but the company doesn't just survive by creating and distributing its well-known products. The company puts an emphasis on innovation, and occasionally an idea takes on new life of its own. In 2013, Coca-Cola marketer AJ Brustein and his coworker Yong Kim set out to help the company solve some of its core workforce challenges. In order to supply the physical products to thousands of different locations, Coca-Cola needed to have staffing plans ready to support packing, delivering, and stocking those products.

In reality, it's not nearly as easy and straightforward as that might sound. People who call in sick, have other personal needs, or who quit without notice can leave the company in a bind, and **every product not ready for purchase is a dollar of revenue the company can't realize**. Brustein and Kim developed Wonolo (which is short for Work Now Locally) as a solution to this.

Wonolo, which has since spun out into its own company and is managed independently, is an on-demand staffing tool that allows companies to "push a button and have someone show up to do a task," as Brustein once put it. Wonolo goes through the paces of finding and preparing potential workers with training and basic qualification, and a store owner can find someone to work on demand as needed. Think of it as just in time labor. For a sense of the scale of this effort, the Wonolo team supports a job seeker database of more than 300,000 workers.

While this isn't meant to establish or maintain a long-term employment relationship, for those people who prefer the flexibility and autonomy of running their own schedule, this helps them to find work when and where it fits their needs while also fulfilling a basic demand for the business as well.

Most importantly, this entire idea came from looking at an existing and very real pain point for many businesses with frontline staff: scheduling and staffing. This is an example of one of the many stories where individuals have moved from idea to action, clearly demonstrating the value of supporting and promoting a spirit of entrepreneurialism within the walls of even the most traditional companies.

Case Study: A Naval Captain Resets the Leadership Model and Performance of the *Santa Fe*

Captain David Marquet was nearing the end of his Naval career and was up for reassignment. He hoped that his next and final posting would be a special reward for his many dedicated years of service. Yet he had a surprise in store. His assignment? The *Santa Fe*, which was the worst-performing submarine in the entire fleet.

Upon arrival, Marquet realized that there were some immediate issues. Workers could easily identify problems, but they were hesitant to ever offer up solutions. Other leaders had taught them that they were to wait for orders, not act independently, in a common "leader-follower" model. One day, he accidentally issued an order that was impossible to fulfill, though his crew tried to accomplish it anyway. When asked why they attempted to carry out the order, the answer from the crew was a common one: "Because you told me to."

To revolutionize the thinking on the ship and break the legacy mindset, Marquet instituted the "leader-leader" model, a transformational approach to leadership and performance on an individual and team basis. Instead of waiting for someone to tell them how to take care of issues, workers across the ship began to take ownership over their areas of responsibility, leading from every possible position, function, and focus area. This included everything from clerical positions and cooks to medics, engineers, and other combat-related roles.

A key tenet that Marquet cites as supportive of this transition is curiosity. Instead of constantly pointing out issues or berating crew members, he would ask open-ended questions about their positions, their responsibilities, and how they thought problems could be solved. This not only encouraged workers to take action when necessary, but it showed them a level of trust and support that they had never before perceived.

Amazingly, the *Santa Fe* transitioned away from performing as the worst ship in the fleet, becoming the highest-performing ship in just one year's time.[44]

---

[29] https://www.wsj.com/articles/how-estimates-of-the-gig-economy-went-wrong-11546857000

[30] https://money.cnn.com/2017/05/24/news/economy/gig-economy-intuit/index.html.

[31] https://www.pewresearch.org/internet/2021/12/08/the-state-of-gig-work-in-2021/

[32] https://cepr.net/we-re-not-all-going-to-be-gig-economy-workers-after-all/

[33]

http://web.archive.org/web/20210909113029/https://2q72xc49mze8bkcog2f01nl h-wpengine.netdna-ssl.com/wp-content/uploads/2015/01/BSG_Uber_Report.pdf

[34] https://www.mckinsey.com/featured-insights/diversity-and-inclusion/race-in-the-workplace-the-frontline-experience

[35] https://www.reuters.com/world/us/exclusive-us-labor-secretary-says-most-gig-workers-should-be-classified-2021-04-29/

[36] https://lhra.io/blog/data-preview-the-great-resignation-nope-its-the-great-reprioritization-new-research/

[37] https://www.census.gov/econ/bfs/data.html

[38] https://sbecouncil.org/about-us/facts-and-data

[39] https://www.evoma.com/business-centre/sme-sector-in-india-statistics-trends-reports/

[40] https://www.gov.uk/government/statistics/business-population-estimates-2022/business-population-estimates-for-the-uk-and-regions-2022-statistical-release-html

[41] https://www.commerceinstitute.com/new-businesses-started-every-year/

[42] https://eig.org/new-start-ups-break-record-in-2021-unpacking-the-numbers/

[43] https://lhra.io/blog/3-frontline-worker-trends-salary-shortage-and-support/

[44] https://davidmarquet.com/turn-the-ship-around-book/

Section 2:
Solutions to Talent Scarcity

5

FINDING, ATTRACTING, AND HIRING WORKERS IN INNOVATIVE WAYS

I was sweating. **Big time**. It was the biggest challenge in my career to date, and I didn't think I would be able to make it happen. There were five or six people in the world qualified to fly this thing, and I had to convince one of them to quit their job and accept an offer with our company. But this wasn't just any aircraft—it was the Special Operations CV-22 vertical takeoff aircraft. A quick Google search will show you what this unique craft looks like, but essentially this aircraft can take off vertically like a helicopter, adjust the rotor position midair, and fly forward as fast as an airplane to its destination. This created incredible maneuverability and flexibility in where it could land and how quickly it could arrive compared to traditional means of shuttling people back and forth between planes and helicopters depending on the need.

Oh, and I had to hire the first person ever to train pilots on these aircraft in a private contractor setting. The problem? The pool of qualified pilots was so small that the price tag to hire them was exorbitant. No, really. There were approximately six people on the planet qualified to do the job, and we had to hire one, fast.

Spoiler alert: I ended up filling the role with an amazing pilot, **but it wasn't because of the money**. We paid him well, yes, but the thing that excited him was the mission and the novelty of this program. He wanted a hand in shaping the future of instruction for this new (but increasingly used) aircraft. In my conversations with him, I found that his professional desire as one of relatively few Latino pilots was to blaze a trail for others to follow. His pioneering spirit was what drove him to pursue training in the aircraft for himself, and that same lever was what I used to help paint a picture of the countless pilots he would be able to instruct and support over the duration of his training career.

Today, he's still training pilots in that aircraft, and he will always have the distinction of being the first ever private pilot to that. It's something that nobody can take away.

In my days as a recruiter, I learned so many incredible lessons about humans, from motivations and drivers to the desire for meaning and purpose. If we're being truthful, not a single one of us has ever taken a job thinking, "I really hope there's no purpose in this work. I really just want to get paid and not have any lasting benefit or value created from coming to work every day."

Sometimes we find a job that meets the many needs we have for meaningful work, validation, and professional satisfaction. Other times we are missing one or more of those, either in the work or the relationships themselves. What I found with recruiting is that we need to find a way to support as many of those needs as possible if we want to create a compelling, competitive offer that people want to consider.

Within this chapter I want to explore a variety of stories and examples that will help to illuminate creative and valuable recruiting practices. In my work I get the benefit of seeing and hearing some amazing stories, and I've done my best to draw out some with some unique approaches we can all learn from. Note that this isn't your standard "follow up with candidates" or "post your jobs on multiple job boards" kind of stuff.

I would hope that many of you are already using those common practices to reach your candidates, engage them as real humans and not just a two-dimensional resume, and convert them into hires. In some cases, these ideas are radical departures from what we might expect hiring to be about. In others, we're reminded of those deep human needs that we must keep in mind if we want to have a successful recruiting practice, regardless of how scarce or plentiful our sources of talent may be.

Hiring in the Talent Crunch of 2021/2022

In a new research study, our team found that eight in 10 talent leaders say that within the last year or two, their recruiting activities have risen from a talent/HR priority to a business/operational level priority as employers have struggled to find and hire enough qualified people. Government data points have continuously demonstrated throughout recent history that the number of job openings have hovered at approximately twice the number of available workers in the United States, which is a recipe for stress and operational risk for every company that is running short-staffed.

As if that wasn't enough, when a labor market gets that tight, it also creates a supply problem for talent acquisition professionals as well. Data from labor market intelligence firm Greenwich.HR from early 2022 showed that the number of job postings for recruiters swelled by more than 5x since pre-pandemic days. Essentially, employers were often finding it difficult to hire the people who do the business of hiring.

While the economy may ebb and flow between cycles of prosperity and contraction, the labor market for recruiting talent is a leading indicator of what the overall hiring market will be. When the United States hiring spree kicked off in Q3 of 2021, recruiter job openings and pay both began to increase. The talented individuals who find the talent companies need to hire are uniquely skilled individuals that are sometimes taken for granted, but over the course of recent history they have been appreciated (and sought after) like never before.

As the talent crunch increased, employers started to notice that their talent teams weren't immune to the wave of resignations that were plaguing them in other areas of the business. In fact, word of offers that were wildly above market rates for recruiter talent were being shared more and more often as fast-growing companies scooped them up to keep the pace of business from slowing. Wild stories about recruiters getting paid $200,000+ with just a few years of experience were commonplace.

One way organizations were elevating the priority of talent acquisition within the business is through higher recruiter compensation. According to data from labor market intelligence company Greenwich.HR, pay rates for recruiting talent increased between 2020 and 2022, and job postings for recruiters spiked off the charts.

Below is a time-based comparison of three different common recruiter job titles (recruiter, senior technical recruiter, and talent acquisition director), how the demand for those individuals has changed over time, and how pay has fluctuated as well based on data drawn from Greenwich.HR's WageScape tools.

Recruiter Job Postings

Recruiter: the basic role of a recruiter can vary widely depending on the company, industry, hiring cycle, and more. We see a wide dispersion in the pay rates for recruiters as low as $20,000 and as high as $100k-plus.

Median salary as of July 2022: $56,500. There was a steady increase in the median since November 2020.

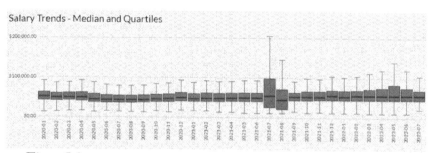

Figure 5.1

Job posting volume: 275,207 since January 2020, with massive spikes in the 12-month period from July 2021 to July 2022. These jobs were posted by 42,000 companies. The number of postings peaked in April 2022 but remained high through the end of July 2022.

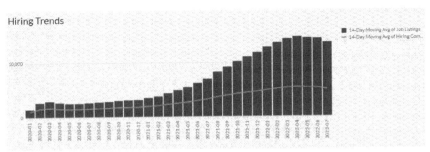

Figure 5.2

Senior Technical Recruiter Job Postings

Senior Technical Recruiter: technical recruiters were in high demand as more companies grew their technology teams, and even with some recent stories of layoffs and/or hiring freezes, job posting volume for senior technical recruiters in July 2022 was still about where it was through the first quarter of 2021 before it began spiking off the charts.

Median salary as of July 2022: $102,500. For comparison purposes, the median rate was $82,500 in June 2021 and $ 78,500 in June 2020.

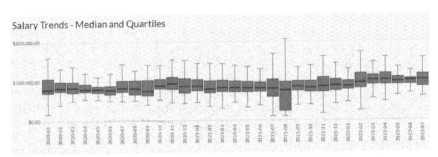

Figure 5.3

Job posting volume: 8,479 listings since January 2020, with the similar July 2021 to July 2022 elevated volume we're seeing across all recruiting roles. The number one hiring entity for these roles? Amazon.

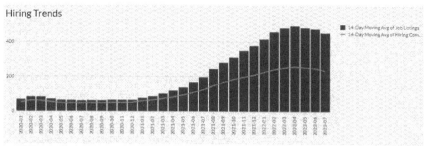

Figure 5.4

Talent Acquisition Director Job Postings

Talent Acquisition Director: Every team needs direction and leadership, and these leaders help to build strategy and align recruiting operations for maximum efficiency and effectiveness.

Median salary as of July 2022: $134,375. Companies flooded the market with openings in July and August of 2021, but overall, the median has continued to rise for these positions, especially in Q2 2022.

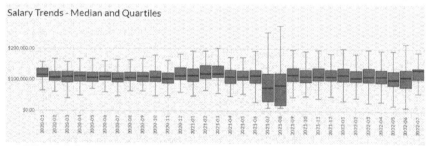

Figure 5.5

Job posting volume: 5,525 jobs were posted by more than 2,500 companies.

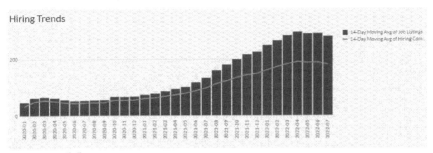

Figure 5.5

On a note related to the previous chapter on gigs and the business boom, we can't easily see the numbers but the high demand for recruiters combined with the increased business startups likely has some correlation. In other words, some number of those companies starting up are for staffing firms or contract recruiters, and it's likely that the percentage of those is higher simply due to the demand. In a news article about technical recruiter layoffs, one Docusign recruiter specifically said that when hiring at the company began to slow in 2022, the person opened up their own contract recruiting firm to make ends meet at home.[45] This is a very common story in the industry where it's relatively easy to set up shop as a sole proprietor with virtually no startup cost.

On the opposite end of the spectrum, when fears of a recession began to circulate in the US in Q3 of 2022, recruiter job openings and pay fell most heavily in those industries affected by layoffs (software and technology). Pay listed on job postings for recruiters fell by 3% between August and November 2022, and it fell by 3x that specifically for technical recruiters (down from $98k to $89k median salary). When fears of that recession pass, recruiter job postings and pay will increase again, and employers will try to catch up on hiring. Unfortunately for my friends in the recruiting profession, this scenario can leave even the most capable and qualified talent acquisition professionals feeling in a state of being perpetually behind and always running to catch up.

Not only that, but in that same hiring research we performed, we noticed that "adding recruiting headcount" was at the bottom of the list in terms of employer plans to mitigate their current hiring challenges. Number one on that list? Adding new hiring tools and technology. We'll cover the technology side of things more extensively in Chapter 7, but that helps to put it into perspective. When we run out of people, we start to look at other options to help us achieve our goals, including a series of choices from outside service providers (contract staffing, recruitment process outsourcing, etc.) to technologies (sourcing, screening, scheduling, and other tools) to help us close the gap.

Importing Global Talent

You may notice that I haven't spent a lot of time talking about things like importing talent from other countries (work visas and immigration), though that is a short-term fix for the companies that want to pursue it. That said, there are already millions of immigrants in the U.S. that are waiting on work visas to be able to take an existing job.[46] Tackling that backlog and streamlining that process could unlock a number of workers for jobs that desperately need to be filled.

In a conversation with one of the leading economists at Indeed, a job board aggregator that receives more than 300 million visitors a month, he explained that when there is a labor shortage, the fastest way to change that is to increase immigration. It's a short-term fix because it doesn't solve some of the other demographic problems raised earlier in this book, but it can work. However, in the last few years, more US-based companies than ever have simply hired workers from other countries, often using online platforms that have proliferated in the era of remote work (Deel, Papaya Global, Oyster, etc.). This lets the individual worker stay home instead of trying to uproot them from their lives for the purpose of taking a job. This is a potential option for those hiring in more corporate-type roles. It also turns out to be a more flexible option that doesn't lock employers into longer-term decisions, visa applications and costs, and relocation logistics for those workers.

Some countries are attempting to establish programs at a national level to attract talent into the region. For example, Germany introduced the Chancenkarte (which literally translates to "opportunity card") as a way to try to appeal to more skilled workers.[47]

While there is debate on whether the specific criteria to receive one of these work visas are the proper ones, it's a clear step in the direction of trying to draw in talent. In Germany's case, this card is available to those **looking** for work, whereas many work visas around the globe require a job offer or some other formal employment contract in order to receive government approval to work. Three out of four specific criteria for the Chancenkarte must be met in order to be eligible:

1) A university degree or professional qualification
2) Professional experience of at least three years
3) Language skill or previous residence in Germany
4) Aged under 35

Again, whether these are the "correct" criteria or not isn't the question. In my mind, I'm curious how long it will take for governments worldwide to begin courting talent the same way companies have for decades. Some are stepping up their game in this area, with Barbados and Bermuda appealing to remote workers with temporary work visas, and Estonia specifically offers a "digital nomad" visa for those workers who live a more travel-heavy lifestyle and work remotely. While it's happening on a more casual scale currently, it will likely heat up as more and more countries struggle to find enough people to fill their critical jobs.

Within the United States, there are even municipalities and localities that are using this "come work here" approach to bring in workers, families, and their associated tax revenue. The city of Greensburg, Indiana offers a $5,000 benefit to newcomers to help them integrate into the local community. For those looking for more options on the extreme ends of the weather spectrum, Juneau, Alaska and Honolulu, Hawaii both offer local incentives ranging from $2,500 to $3,000 to attract workers.

Okay, that's enough about immigration for now. Let's start looking at some of the practical and tangible things employers should be doing to appeal to job seekers in a talent shortage.

Knowing (and Showing) Your Full Value as an Employer

Recruiting and analytics expert Trent Cotton, VP of Recruiting and Culture at HatchWorks, tells a powerful story about what it means to inspire a bigger vision when we talk to our candidates. Consider the two stories below and which one inspires you:

Story #1: See that wooden bench over there? It's sitting on the main sidewalk out in front of the college campus and has been for years. Right now, the campus maintenance board is deliberating on whether to tear it down. Would you be willing to donate some money to save it?

Story #2: See that wooden bench over there? It's dedicated in memory to Susan Green who passed away from cancer during her time as a student here. Every time people walk by, they touch it and see it as a symbol of hope and persistence in the face of overwhelming obstacles. Susan has touched and inspired so many students to push through the challenges in front of them so they can ultimately succeed. The campus maintenance board is deliberating on whether to tear it down. Would you be willing to donate some money to save it?

All of us, with little prompting, would easily pick the second story here as one that inspires us to action. Cotton's focus with this example is to remind us that we can be selling a job and a pay rate (Story #1), or we can be selling a bigger vision, meaning, and impact (Story #2) when we talk with candidates from a recruiting perspective. In recent years more companies have thought critically about their employer value proposition (EVP) and how it is communicated. Your EVP includes everything you have to offer to a prospective hire, not just the dollars you are trading for their time and effort. For example, if someone works for a nonprofit, that individual nearly always expects to be paid slightly less than work in the private sector in exchange for working for a mission-oriented organization.

In healthcare, patient-centricity is everything. In fact, the CEO of Scripps Health once said that during orientation, the team brings in a former patient who tells their personal story of what the hospital's care and staff meant to them. If the nursing candidates seeing and hearing that story weren't brought to tears, he had the hiring team double check to make sure if they were the right people for the job.

Admittedly, not every company has a clear emotional connection to tap into like those examples, but there are often ways to create a sense of connectedness and meaning. For instance, GATR Technologies was founded in Huntsville, Alabama in 2004. In 2005 when Hurricane Katrina devastated the Gulf Coast, the founder of GATR packed up his prototype mobile satellite in his personal vehicle and drove down to Louisiana. Upon arrival, he launched the mobile communications device into the air and began supporting local logistics for nonprofits and other organizations, enabling communications and helping people to mobilize relief efforts and supplies.

That powerful story of helping people during the toughest of times? It was shared during orientation with every new hire by the company's HR manager in an effort to create a deeper and more meaningful connection to the company's mission of enabling communications for everyone, especially in difficult situations.

I'll share one final example of this to avoid being overly repetitive. In a discussion with Kelly Burlage, VP of Talent Acquisition for Lineage Logistics, she told me that the company wasn't just a temperature-controlled shipping company. Instead, she points out that Lineage is helping to ensure that healthy, fresh food is delivered anywhere people need it in the world. If I was trying to attract quality talent to work for Lineage, I'd choose the latter description, too.

Bottom line: if you haven't given thought to this yet, it's an important point to consider weaving not just into your interviews and recruiting conversations, but into your career site, outreach messages, and other communications throughout the hiring process. Whether you tell your story or not matters. How you tell your story matters. We all want to know that the work we are doing matters on a grander scale. If you can help your candidates and workforce see how they play a part in that bigger story and how they are impacting lives in a positive way, your business will reap the benefits.

Giving Everyone Their Fair Chance

In the United States, more than two million people are currently incarcerated. That number climbs to more than 10 million when we look at a global perspective. On top of that, nearly one in three Americans (an estimated 70 to 100 million people) have some sort of criminal record. In the last few years, U.S. employers have increased their focus on this population, with job site Indeed reporting that fair chance hiring ads were up 31% between 2019 and 2022.[48] However, this still only accounts for about 3% of all job postings at its peak, which is why it's such a big opportunity for employers to consider. As a comparison benchmark, Indeed also reported that searches by job seekers for fair chance opportunities were up 117% over that same time period.

Affected individual often have trouble finding work after serving a prison term, further complicating their lives. But employers that are willing to consider hiring these individuals can potentially change the direction of someone's life dramatically, as the following stories show.

Hot Chicken Takeover is a regional restaurant chain known to its customers for its spicy and delicious chicken. To its staff, it's known as a second chance at life. To the founder, Joe DeLoss, hiring and changing lives was his primary mission: chicken was just the means to an end. In an interview with the social entrepreneur, he shared that his focus was on growing a business that could allow individuals with a history of incarceration, homelessness, and other employment barriers to get their own shot at doing good work. It has paid off, as the company has grown to hundreds of employees, multiple locations, and legions of raving fans who love the food and atmosphere. DeLoss also tailors the company's benefits to meet the needs of this unique workforce. He said that he quickly learned that many of the workers couldn't plan for retirement or longer-term goals because they had immediate financial barriers, so he supports a matching savings program to help workers save for housing, education, and personal transportation. Unlike most food service locations where turnover often runs 75% a year (in other words, three in four workers leave annually), Hot Chicken Takeover has a

retention rate of 75%, keeping the majority of staff year over year.

The success of this company, in DeLoss' mind, comes down to giving people a chance who had previously been prevented from gaining meaningful employment. However, Hot Chicken Takeover isn't the only company to push the boundaries on this concept. The idea of fair chance hiring isn't new, but it's continued to evolve in recent years as more companies want to unblock hiring obstacles for these workers. In the words of one talent professional I interviewed recently, "It's not about lowering the bar, it's about lowering the barriers to employment."

One company that takes this approach even further is Greyston Bakery. Known for their incredible brownies, the company has a motto that says it all: *we don't hire people to bake brownies. We bake brownies to hire people.* Greyston's approach to hiring is a novel one that it refers to as "open hiring." Essentially, anyone with any kind of background can apply with Greyston, and when an opening comes available, that person gets an offer. There are no resumes, no screening processes, and no barriers to entry. The company believes in this approach so strongly that it set up a separate employer training program to help other businesses learn how to hire and develop staff the Greyston way. This concept is one that appeals broadly, based on recent news—one international company that is leveraging the Open Hiring concept is IKEA. The 225,000-employee home furnishing company has plans to implement the approach for North America hiring to further support its goals for more equitable hiring processes.

One final story to round out this conversation comes from an Arizona-based firm called Televerde. Julie Salomone, the company's Vice President of Global Human Resources, recently shared about the company's innovative approach to giving people a second chance. While the stories above demonstrated opportunities to support individuals after being released from prison, Televerde has worked to hire women **actively serving terms** within correctional facilities in the US and UK, providing valuable work experiences and a chance to save money for a life after prison.[49]

Salomone pointed out that her passion comes from investing in people and investing in employees. There are only so many ways that you can reward people with money, but for this specific segment of the workforce, a valuable currency is skills. That's why Televerde employment prioritizes skill development in the women it supports, giving them a chance to build up their professional development and future work opportunities. However, she also points out that there's a deeper human value to this as well, as the work creates more self-esteem for the women and gives them a purpose when they often feel like they don't have one. That said, it's not assumed that this is just going to work without effort. In Salomone's words, "Even women in prison have choices, and we want to make sure that we are an employer of choice and that we're giving back to them as much as they're giving to us." Similar to Greyston's training approach, Televerde supports the Televerde Foundation to teach its principles to other organizations that want to follow in its footsteps.

Each of these stories serve as examples to show that the millions of people affected by these circumstances have value to offer, and employers who are willing to take a chance on these individuals will find out what Hot Chicken Takeover, Greyston, and other firms know all too well: believing in someone when nobody else will creates lasting loyalty in an employment relationship while changing lives for the better.

If Everyone Else is Doing It, Try Something Else

A few months ago during a research roundtable, I had the opportunity to meet with seven heads of HR and talent acquisition for firms representing millions of employees collectively. The discussions ranged from what was working to what was causing untold amounts of frustration, but one story stood out as an innovative way to solve one of the most common labor shortages: nurses.

Depending on the source, estimates on the shortage of qualified nurses in coming years span 200,000 to nearly 500,000 workers. This shortage is caused by numerous factors, and it has spawned a travel nursing industry where some nurses become a mercenary-like workforce, moving from place to place based on who pays the most. One nurse told me that she made more than $400,000 in 2020 in base and overtime pay, and a healthcare financial executive told me that his health system is actually losing money on its travel nursing costs but making the funds up elsewhere in the budget just to have enough staff to operate. In short: it's a strange and different experience compared to the typical work environment most of us are accustomed to.

In the research forum, the HR executive for the healthcare system employing 80,000-plus staff outlined a recent "recruiting field trip" to a United States territory. The approach was nothing short of brilliant.

The recruiting team met with the entire graduating class of nurses at one university, offering them each a one-year contract at a hospital in the United States. This offered multiple benefits to the workers, including higher pay scales and a guaranteed position upon graduation. The company also benefited as well, and not just by filling roles critical to the business. For instance, because this was a territory of the United States, there were no troublesome issues with immigration or work visas, and every one of the graduates spoke excellent English as well. Ultimately a large percentage of the nursing students agreed to take the contracts, signing up on the spot.

What I love most about this story is that while other organizations continue to struggle to pay the spiraling costs of travel nurses and hiring bonuses for more traditional nurse hires, this healthcare system looked in a different direction and was able to scoop up qualified graduates at a more moderate pay scale.

Speaking of acquiring a targeted group of graduates, one way to do this more strategically is with educational partnerships. A key lever for creating more skilled workers and developing a capable workforce is through education—both technical and traditional higher education channels. While some companies are doing a great job of interacting with and establishing feeder programs for their talent through educational partners, it's still not as common as one might think. While this isn't a central point in the book, it's something that we recommend employers consider as a strategy. For instance, having personal relationships with key professors at a local college can help to steer high performers toward your organization in an informal way.

However, it's also worth looking at more strategic partnerships as well. In my own city, several auto manufacturers have set up plant operations in recent years, and many of our community colleges now have certificate programs that qualify someone to take a well-paying job after completion of the coursework and hands-on training experiences. This kind of relationship isn't just for massive enterprise companies. If your organization hires a number of people each year, then this could serve as a valuable channel for skilled workers. Unlike more traditional degree programs, these certificates are often developed in conjunction with the employer based on the job tasks and responsibilities, ensuring minimal on the job training post-hire. Education is an important lever for increasing the number of people who are able to work and fill critical roles over the long term.

Let's take a step over into another common industry—financial services. If you're working in that space, how could you break some of the commonly held beliefs that might hold your organization back from critical hires? In a discussion with one of the heads of staffing at Northwestern Mutual, we looked at some of the company's profiles it targets for one of its roles with higher volume.[50] Instead of doing what virtually every other company does when hiring for a position, which is looking at people with who have previous experience in the role, the team took a different approach. In a brainstorming meeting, one of the recruiters realized that one profession kept showing up in high-performing hires for this particular role year after year. That unlikely profession? Teaching.

So, from that point forward, the team began to create strategic plans to target teachers who were burned out or ready for a new and different challenge. They went where teachers went, spent time in communities where teachers gathered, and understood what kinds of hot buttons teachers might have that drive them away from their jobs. With that depth and breadth of intelligence, the team took action, and the plan enabled the company to fill a significant percentage of its roles with diverse individuals who had backgrounds similar to other high-performing hires.

Our last example of trying something unpredictable comes from an organization that we'd expect to be bureaucratic, old-fashioned, and over-the-top conservative in how it operates. The Federal Bureau of Investigation is a US government entity with more than 35,000 employees in roles covering everything as diverse as linguists and field agents to scientists, IT professionals, and accountants. While it's very easy to look at traditional backgrounds when hiring, we all realize that hiring the same profile repeatedly can cause blind spots over time. In an interview during one of our talent acquisition-focused virtual events, FBI talent acquisition leader Peter Sursi talked about his perspective on the topic, bringing up a way to provide more opportunities for diverse individuals while also opening up hiring to new and untapped sources of talent. In essence, the focus is on hiring people with **potential**, even if they don't have the exact list of required experiences at the moment they are selected. What Peter (and many of us) have found is pretty straightforward when you think about it: hiring someone who wants to work and succeed can outweigh someone's greater skills or knowledge in some cases. While I don't want to hire an untrained brain surgeon only because they are enthusiastic, I can hire for many other positions based on someone's willingness to work, learn, and adapt.

Most organizational concerns when it comes to hiring are focused on risk. If we hire this person, we are potentially risking poor performance. That's why we hire based on a template for what worked in the past—to reduce the risk of picking the wrong person. But the problem is when we start to hire people that are so much alike that they all share the same blind spots. In Peter's words, there's another risk we should be taking instead: "Why not risk hiring someone amazing?"

There's some interesting research to back this up. In 2019, David Epstein authored a popular book called *Range*. The book looks at the importance of having a range of skills within a person to make them more capable while also creating a level of adaptability and resilience to change. One of the stories that stands out to me from the book was about two different life sciences teams that were trying to solve a similar problem. One team was made up of the same types of specialists (microbiologists, for example) and the second team was a mixture of specialties (microbiologist, epidemiologist, hematologist, etc.) The second group was able to solve the problem much more rapidly because each person had a different piece of the puzzle, while each member of the first group (to continue the metaphor) was carrying around the exact same puzzle piece. This concept is exactly what Sursi is talking about when it comes to hiring. If we're only hiring the same people we've always hired, we will only be able to solve the kinds of problems we have solved in the past, not the new and different ones coming down the line.

Hiring The People You Already Hired (Again)

It's been shown over the years that one of the highest quality sources of hire is one of your alumni—someone who worked for your company previously and left on good terms. Often called "boomerang" employees, these workers know your business, already have social connections within the company, and can more quickly ramp up than someone joining the company without those prior ties. Dr. John Sullivan is a globally recognized thinker and researcher on the topic, and his work has shown time and time again that boomerang hires are some of the highest quality sources that exist.[51] There are various approaches to this. For example, Sodexo, which employs more than 400,000 workers globally, has a formal alumni network called Reconnexions. Members of this group can access additional job opportunities not available on the public external careers site, professional development resources, a network of talent professionals, and more. Sodexo had more than 9,000 individuals in its alumni network in 2020, which means quick access to talent that has already proven ready and willing to work at the company in the past.[52]

A more specific example of alumni hiring is from a North American engineering and aerospace company. When the firm's People team realized that they had lost a significant number of women from their workforce (primarily due to caregiver responsibilities) over the course of 2020 and 2021, the company decided to see if those individuals were willing to come back to work. However, instead of just calling them and asking for them to consider rejoining the firm, the aerospace company's talent acquisition team took a more strategic approach.

First, recruiting leaders looked through the employee population to find other women that had left and returned. If they were comfortable with it, each of those women were asked to tell their stories about why they left and why they returned, their fears and concerns, and what reality was like for them upon rejoining the firm.

Next, the recruiting team created a communications campaign around those stories, targeting the women in their database who had left work during that timeframe since there was a high probability that they left for the same reasons. Instead of trying to cajole and convince those women, they let their peers with the same experiences do the heavy lifting by sharing their own stories.

Imagine being on the receiving end of this messaging campaign. You're a woman who left work because you couldn't or didn't want to have to balance virtual/remote school for your elementary-age children with a full workload, and you don't know if you'll ever be able to return to the job you did previously. Then you get this message from a woman in the company that you respect talking about her own fears and concerns on the topic of balancing work and life and what it was like for her to transition back to full-time employment.

Alumni, or boomerang, hiring is a powerful tool both en masse and in a more strategic sense. It's very common to hear stories about people leaving a job and finding out that it wasn't what they hoped for. In our 2022 research on frontline workers, we actually saw that about half of them that changed jobs regretted it for a variety of reasons. Having an alumni network can help to find opportunities to transition those individuals back into the workforce instead of losing access to them permanently.

Targeting Experienced Workers

I still remember hiring Bill. This gentleman was in his 70s, and we were hiring for a technical writer to join our team. The hurdle? Bill's wife. See, we had offered him a position that was in line with his pay expectations and fit his skills perfectly, but his wife was concerned about Bill driving to the office in the winter because it became dark earlier and he sometimes had trouble driving in those conditions. I called his wife and asked her to come by the office so we could talk. I showed her where Bill would be working, introduced her to some of the team, and did a quick tour of the office. She was still worried about the commute, so I shared the detail I had been holding in reserve: we had flexible hours. As long as Bill got his work done, he could come in earlier and leave earlier, avoiding the dark hours of driving and any danger that may potentially pose. She immediately lit up in a smile and took his arm, saying, "You better not quit. These are **nice** people."

I love that story because it shows a few critical things. First, workers who are older or more experienced may have different needs than those at the other end of the age spectrum. The 24-year old employee may instead need a bit of flexibility for childcare drop-offs, for instance. However, if we can find a way to make it work, we get the benefit of someone who has a wealth of experience to share both formally in work products and informally in mentorship of their peers.

Recent research shows that the number of people in the U.S. workforce aged 75 and older will increase by 96.5% in 2030.[53] Some employers are already looking at how to lure these workers in with a variety of programs and approaches. We already saw in Chapter Three how Aerospace Corp is approaching this strategic source of talented workers, but here are a few that we can learn from.

- AlliedUniversal employs more than 800,000 workers globally in security and facility services positions. In a podcast interview with one of their talent executives, I learned about the company's partnerships with AARP (The American Association of Retired Persons) and other community organizations to target and hire older workers. AlliedUniversal offers referral bonus payments to these organizations for qualified hires.[54]

- CVS employs more than 300,000 workers across the United States at nearly 10,000 locations. The company has instituted a "snowbird" program as part of its *Talent is Ageless* strategy. Pharmacists in northern states can migrate south to more comfortable temperatures during cold weather months.[55]

- British airline easyJet is targeting workers in their later stages of life for cabin crew positions. The company's data show that more than half of British adults over 45 years old want to explore a new career after their children leave home. easyJet is using some of its existing workforce in that age demographic in its recruitment advertising to support the campaign and help other individuals visualize themselves in similar roles.[56]

It's easy to see why companies are pursuing these individuals. They have significant work and life experiences they can bring to bear, and they are more likely to be loyal and supportive when they see others like them that are already succeeding in the workplace.

The Role of Talent Intelligence

Between 2021 and 2022 when the hiring market was in a frenzy, we saw a massive uptick in the number of companies using what we call talent intelligence. This includes a combination of data on labor markets, skill supply and demand statistics, and pay insights. I'll be clear: talent intelligence doesn't create new skilled talent for you to hire. However, it may help to uncover where those skilled individuals exist, what they cost, and how many you can hire.

Companies have been using this type of information for years. In one conversation with John Healy, managing partner for the Center for the Transformation of Work, he explained how he had worked with large employers over the years on site selection for new business units and operations. John's focus is on talent acquisition, but by gathering enough data, he could help pinpoint where those organizations could open a facility that required 2,000 staff where they would be able to afford the talent and find enough qualified workers at the same time.

It's clear how that kind of information has value at a macro level, but it also plays out on a micro level as well. We are seeing more technology providers that try to use talent intelligence for sourcing individual jobs, understanding competitive pay, and targeting skilled talent. It's important to note that this kind of approach is most valuable when demand for talent is high. That's why we saw so many companies trying to launch their own talent intelligence function in recent years. As I've pointed out a few times, even if the economy ebbs and flows, the overall scarcity of talent means taking steps towards understanding and building out some talent intelligence capabilities is an investment in long-term hiring success.

In a recent discussion with a talent intelligence leader for a company with more than 50,000 employees, we looked at the leader's plans for standing up its own talent intelligence function internally. Their team is bringing in data from both government and industry sources to help with daily decisions as well as longer term strategic ones. The hardest balance, in their words, is balancing between strategic and tactical. Getting too nuanced means getting too busy to do all of the work necessary. Being too high level means the information will never really serve as intelligence for the frontline recruiters that are looking for candidates on a daily basis.

This talent intelligence approach will continue to evolve, but I see it playing a critical role in how companies seek out talent, especially when talent is scarce.

Throughout this chapter we have explored numerous examples and situations to make hiring smarter and more targeted. You hopefully have a few ideas percolating in your mind that will serve as key ingredients for hiring success in the coming months and years, but we're not done yet.

In the next chapter you will learn both emerging and time-tested strategies for retaining a high-quality workforce. I encourage you to look at them in conjunction with your recruiting strategy, because **the easiest job to fill is one where you don't lose the person in the first place**. In other words, every person you can retain is one less person you have to hire.

Case Study: Audible's Innovative Approach to Bring Caregivers Back to the Workforce

If you've ever provided care for a child, parent, or other family member, you know how all-consuming it can be. When that season of caregiving is over, the person who has poured their heart and soul into serving someone else is most often left with a gap on their resume that can harm their attempts to rejoin the workforce. Audible has taken the approach that these individuals are to be celebrated and supported, not looked down upon for their lack of recent work experience. The company established a "Next Chapter" Returnship program that helps to transition caregivers back into the workforce by giving them useful, valuable work and helps the company determine if they want to hire the individual full time after the program runs its course.

The program is the brainchild of Supriya Mimani, Audible's director of HR programs. Mimani has said in numerous interviews that data show that women are much likelier to put their careers on hold, which makes re-entering the workforce even more prohibitive—especially in the always-changing tech field. It's frustrating to see this amazing pool of talented people being kept from working for no other reason than taking a short career break to care for a loved one.

To tap into that pool of people, Mimani worked with leadership and several teams across the company to launch Audible's "Next Chapter" Returnship Program in October 2020. The 16-week program was available to mid-career professionals with more than a year's gap in their experience and offered the possibility of full-time employment at the end.

In February 2021, the inaugural returnship group was hired as part of Audible's partnership with the nonprofit Path Forward. By Mimani's design, a virtual army of people stepped in to onboard the group to Audible: their new managers, a group mentor, human resources representatives, and team "buddies." Senior Vice President of Technology Mike Masiello, who had been championing the program at every turn, had an hour-long lunch with each individual to get to know them better, and Chief Technology Officer Tim Martin, along with other leaders, made sure to speak with the group within their first two days. Employee-led impact groups like Women in Tech and Moms@Audible led interactive sessions on imposter syndrome, confidence, work-life balance, and more. One participant reported, "I didn't feel like I was getting back to work after a decade, nor did the team treat me that way."

Amid all these layers of support, the returnship group started a Slack channel and quickly became close. The channel soon filled with questions and advice on anything from acronyms and esoteric terms used by certain teams to how to use their new remote-productivity tools. This was also a secret hope of Mimani at the beginning of the program, as she counted on them forming tight bonds to help them weather the inevitable struggles faced by returning to the workplace.

Next Chapter's pilot program was such a success that Audible began tripling the number of returnships available and extending opportunities into marketing and data science, as well as tech.

> ### Case Study: Delta Airlines Shows Candidates They are Valued and Appreciated

Delta Airlines employs more than 90,000 workers across its various business units, from flight operations to technology and everything in between. One of the company's talent acquisition leaders recently told me on a podcast interview that thousands of people click over from Delta's consumer-facing website to its careers page every year.[57] Because every potential hire is also a potential customer, Delta's talent acquisition team takes candidate experience very seriously. After all, failing to follow up or engage with a candidate could affect their likelihood of traveling with Delta in the future.

When you think about it, the majority of candidates in a hiring process are set up to be disappointed. After all, dozens of candidates may apply, but typically only one of them is actually selected for the job. Delta created a framework called "Designing for the Disappointed" to ensure that every candidate felt valued and appreciated during the application and screening process.

One key way this was prioritized is through the hiring assessment the firm uses to screen applicants. Many companies use assessments and have for years, but it's often a black box sort of answer for candidates: either you get through or you don't. Delta worked with its assessment provider to create an employer-facing report, which is fairly standard, but they also created a candidate-facing report. That candidate report was streamlined and simplified, and it listed a few of the key strengths of the candidate. **Even if a candidate isn't selected for the job, they still get a copy of those results**. Delta's hiring team has heard stories of candidates taking those results along with a resume to future job applications at other companies, which demonstrates the value that candidates feel when they receive something.

At the core, there's a psychological element to hiring. When we

73

give our highest effort, submit a resume, and hope for the best, yet receive nothing, it can be incredibly frustrating. In this case, even candidates who weren't chosen still have something useful they can take with them. Delta is using this simple, yet effective, approach to increase candidate satisfaction. However, this approach also increases the likelihood that those candidates will reapply to other jobs in the future and continue to see Delta as an air carrier of choice from a consumer perspective.

6

EMPLOYEE RETENTION
IN THE NEW ERA

It was a happy accident, really. I was running a workforce study on benefit choices and had one question slot left to fill. We already had all the necessary questions in the study, so I threw in one that had been on my list for some time. The question: **what does flexibility mean to you as an employee?** See, when we think about this from a talent or business leader perspective, we often think it means **when** someone comes to work or **where** they put their rear end when they are working. And yes, that's a part of it, but it turns out that it's a much smaller part than we think it is.

In the responses from workers, we found that "where I work" ranked number **five** on the list! The number one answer? "More autonomy and control in my job." In a world where news headlines scream about the dangers of not offering remote work or losing out on your entire workforce, the data actually show something very different. In fact, this research question spurred an entire line of questioning simply due to the fact that in the year after COVID first hit, in any conversation about working from home or flexibility, there were a significant number of people in every conversation that said, "Yeah, but we never got to work from home. We've been in the office, on the job site, in the classroom, etc. all along."

What People Actually Want

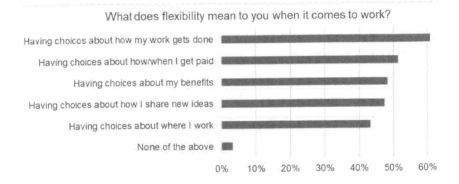

What does flexibility mean to you when it comes to work?

Figure 6.1

That repetitive set of responses planted a seed in my heart. Yes, I said in my heart, and not in my head! See, many times a research question will bounce around my mind until I find the right way to ask it. In this case, I felt deep compassion for those leaders who were trying to run their businesses, hire talent, and keep things working when they didn't have the "remote work" button to push as an option for their staff. While remote and hybrid work aren't easy or without their own challenges, it felt like this group of people, companies, and their entire workforce were left out in the cold, because one of the most often suggested strategies for hiring and retention in those days revolved around allowing workers to work from home.

With that in mind, I dove into this concept of flexibility for nonflexible jobs and industries and came away with a series of ideas and concepts for embedding practical flexibility into work without having to resort to remote work if that wasn't a viable option. I'll get into those later in this chapter, but I tell this story specifically because it illustrates how we have to think differently about employee retention if we are going to be successful long-term.

Often times we think of some of the typical areas like pay or benefits when it comes to employee retention. And those matter. But when compared against some other factors, there may be other low-hanging fruit that employers can use to keep their most valuable team members. Within the context of this chapter, we will explore:

- Pay as a motivator (or not)
- Why flexibility is the best benefit you can offer today
- The top reasons for job quits in the last 18 months
- The single biggest factor in employee loyalty and commitment
- And the powerful role that growth and mobility plays in an employee's intent to stay in a job

Competitive Hiring, Pay, and Other Benefits

In our 2022 Talent Acquisition Trends study, we found that for candidates, the number one priority for them in the hiring process is knowing the starting salary for the position. Pay isn't the only lever that we should be pulling to find new talent, but it's one that we immediately think of when it comes to competition for the best people.

In truth, we saw a glimpse of this in 2021 and 2022 when employers were struggling to find people and in some cases were willing to pay previously unheard-of sums to get them to join or stay. From the common headlines that tracked many retail and food service roles that were paid starting salaries of $15 or $20 an hour to other professions that were in high demand, pay spiked in a significant way. Three out of four employers admitted that pay had been a sticking point in the hiring process for their company over the 2021-2022 period, further illustrating how it rises to the top in a competitive market.

In a discussion with the CHRO for one of the world's largest pizza companies, he told me that unlike pre-COVID times when job offers for an hourly worker of a dollar an hour might or might not entice them to leave a job, COVID broke many local job market economies by shifting the pay scales dramatically. Instead of a dollar an hour, some workers could bump their pay by 50% or 100% with one job change.

Historically, pay has been assumed to be a trigger for leaving by most managers. In the excellent book *7 Hidden Reasons Employees Leave* by Leigh Branham, the author's research from analyzing tens of thousands of data points around employee turnover indicates that managers believe 80% of the reason people leave a job is due to pay. However, the real reasons that make up about 78% of worker decisions to leave (almost the exact inverse) come down to work conditions, manager relationships, culture, career advancement, and other factors. This is in a normal market where pay increases to go from one company to a similar position at another company may be in the 5-10% range. However, when someone is offered a new position with a 30% or higher increase, it breaks the longstanding thinking on this. And that 30% figure isn't just pulled from thin air: data from labor market intelligence company Greenwich.HR indicate that the median advertised salaries rose between June 2020 and January 2021 by 30% nationally.

Think about this on a human level. Consider an individual making $12 an hour in 2020. If they got an offer to make $12.50 from a competitor, they would weigh that decision against the fact that they have a very supportive manager, schedule flexibility, or a position on a leadership track, and they may or may not decide to take that position. Now imagine that same person is offered $20 an hour. That's nearly double the pay, and for someone in that position, it's potentially lifechanging for them and/or their family. Even if they have a great manager or other benefits, they are much more likely to accept that new position. (Not to get off topic, but that exact point may be why we see about half of workers saying they regret their job changes in the last two years. Moving to a new job just to earn more money doesn't lead to long-term satisfaction. When that novelty wears off, regret can set in.)

At some point within the job market, that pace of increases slows down. It can't continue on a breakneck pace forever, and the market eventually returns to its regular, smaller adjustments as people move from company to company. At this point, the more historical model of why people stay or leave a job comes back into play, and workers again turn their attention to some of the tangible and intangible elements of a job other than pay when making a career decision.

To look at this concept from a different angle, we know that pay is a terrible motivator of performance and satisfaction. Yes, for some of you that may be a revelation, but numerous studies show that pay doesn't drive long-term performance. It is better for short-term incentives and goals, especially when someone has a large amount of control over the variables in their work (think sales, for example). For a knowledge worker who is evaluated primarily on the output of their brain, pay isn't a great motivator. What does this have to do with hiring?

In psychology there's a term called the "hedonic treadmill." It has been determined that any one of us has a sort of internal thermostat for happiness, and even if something influences that to change temporarily, it almost always reverts back to that preset level. This has been proven with research on lottery winners (positive change to satisfaction levels) and those that face medical challenges (negative change to satisfaction levels). After the initial change, the happiness settles back to its prior range.[58]

In the workplace, this applies to pay. Researchers have found that once people make above a threshold of compensation (approximately $75,000), they begin to prioritize other factors than just compensation in their decisions, because compensation isn't a primary motivator beyond that pay level.[59]

For an example other than pay, workers like benefits that feel like they are tailored to their own personal situation. For a long time, the benefits employers offered were one-size-fits-all. Healthcare, paid leave, and maybe some disability or life insurance coverage were fairly standard. However, increasingly employers are offering new and different benefits to try to attract and keep talent.

These range extensively from health and wellbeing solutions that help to understand and support the mental and emotional health of the workforce to family care solutions that encompass elder care, childcare, and more. This list can be extensive: pet care offerings, technologies that allow employees to convert paid leave to other benefits, and even smaller company options that support stipends and perks for maximum flexibility. The number of technologies and companies that fit into this classification have expanded rapidly in recent years. In our technology awards program, which reviews dozens of technologies that support employee activities across the employment lifecycle, we've seen a dramatic increase in those classified as employee benefits.

One last comment on the benefits front: in one research initiative, workers told us that **flexibility in the benefits they have ranks higher for them than flexibility in where they work**. That was a surprising finding and reiterates just how important benefits can be. In that same study, we found that most employees would prefer to be able to use some of their accrued paid leave (paid time off, or vacation, depending on what your company calls it) for other purposes. If given the choice, 83% of workers would prefer to convert their leave balance into other financial resources ranging from emergency cash and retirement contributions to student loan repayment and charitable contributions. One company that offers that benefit is PTO Exchange. The Seattle-based company serves employers of varying industries as they look for ways to reward their people, even if they can't use all of their accrued paid time off.

Breaking those preferences out demographically presents us with some logical results: older workers would rather use the funds for retirement savings, and younger workers would be more likely to use it for student loan repayment.

Okay, we can shift away from the benefits discussion for now, but hopefully these varying data points and examples help to illustrate just how important it is not just to offer benefits, but to offer flexible benefits that give workers options. When we compare them against a pay increase that will quickly become "normal" for them, benefits give people a chance to recreate the sense of appreciation and attachment every time they use them.

Flexibility for Nonflexible Jobs and Industries

If you work for a software company, chances are you're one of many people who is working a remote or hybrid schedule these days. The following section is dedicated to people who don't have those options, but there are still some phenomenal ideas related to employee retention that you won't want to miss.

However, if you're in some other industries, your workforce is likely feeling some different emotions because they may not have the option of working virtually. While it's easy to get caught up in the discussion of the companies in the headlines, the truth is many employers (and their workers) don't have the option of working remotely. Their work could be:

- A product created in a physical environment
- A product delivered in a customer-facing environment
- A service delivered in a customer-facing environment

Still not sure what that encompasses? Consider this list:

- Manufacturing
- Construction
- Agriculture
- Mining/Oil/Gas
- Retail
- Food service
- Healthcare
- Utilities
- Public service
- Leisure, hospitality, and travel
- Trucking and logistics

These industries employ nearly two billion frontline workers globally that do not have the option of connecting in and doing their job from a home office. And for years, the conversation/debate has raged around this. In virtually every one of the dozens of speaking events I've participated in over the last year, the moment remote work comes up, the audience divides into the "haves" and "have nots."

If you're one of the leaders who falls on the "have not" side of that equation, I'm going to walk through what these jobs that are not remote-friendly can do to support flexibility at work.

By the way, it's worth noting that the research shows a few things related to this conversation. First, people in all jobs appreciate flexibility, even if it looks different in some jobs, industries, or companies when compared to others. Second, not everyone really does want to work from home, despite what the headlines might indicate. In our Great Reprioritization study, we saw that approximately 60% of workers in any modality (hybrid, in-person, or remote) were happy with their situation. The other 40% were interested in something different as a personal preference. This means we can't make every single person happy, but it also means this discussion around flexibility is powerful for giving each person some choices and options around how their work fits into their life.

One final note before we jump into some ideas: this is definitely focused on employee retention, as it should be, but there's also a hiring element to it as well. I spoke with the Chief Learning Officer for a healthcare organization recently and the person explained that their company has lost dozens of highly talented applicants for functional and back-office roles. That drop off happens during the hiring process within minutes of explaining that the job isn't a remote one. So, while we'd like to segment flexibility off as a different conversation from anything related to hiring, it's definitely linked.

The first thing that we assume as employers is that flexibility means working from the couch in a pair of pajamas.

Stop assuming.

We want to think that flexibility is only about remote or in person or hybrid, because that's what we keep hearing. But it's not. People working in a physical location don't have any illusions that they're going to be driving a forklift, serving a meal, or assembling a refrigerator compressor from their couch. Instead, flexibility is about someone's control and autonomy.

I always advise employers to ask their people what flexibility means to them, because we may have a skewed vision of what that means as business leaders. Or we may think that they want something much more robust and specific than it needs to be. Do not define flexibility for them, instead, let them do it for you.

That said, flexibility has a variety of facets. Even if we must have people working on site because it is a business requirement, we can still offer flexibility in a few critical ways.

1) Control and autonomy options

Give people more control over how their work gets done. Don't lower the bar on what you expect them to produce but do lower your expectations that you can tell them exactly how to do it. Or as I like to put it: tell them **what** they are responsible for but leave the **how** up to them. While some work follows a very specific, required process, many times it does not.

For example, years ago U.S. Cellular was revitalizing its culture after years of letting it fall by the wayside. One of the key aspects in that transformation was increased autonomy and empowerment for front line support staff. In our data we see that frontline workers quit jobs due to burnout and stress more often than nonfrontline workers. It's no wonder: prior to the changes, irate customers would enter the stores with broken phones or other issues, and the associates had to call support to determine acceptable solutions because they were not given the authority to solve any of the problems themselves. Customers couldn't get their phones or billing issues resolved, and workers faced mounting levels of stress because they were essentially helpless to act.

The change that leadership made was a simple one: the retail associates could solve problems for customers as long as the cost was below a certain threshold. No longer did they need to wait for 30 minutes on the phone to get three approvals to replace someone's $99 broken phone. They could just make it right, and they could do it in the moment. Not only did that single change increase customer satisfaction, but it also increased workforce satisfaction as well.

As someone who has spent time running an HR function, I like practical ideas. I'll share with you one of my favorites when it comes to evaluating autonomy and making this a more tangible conversation for managers. It's called an autonomy audit. Essentially, managers and their teams get a chance to rate the autonomy that the employees get on a scale. A "1" score would signify the world's worst micromanager that controls all decisions, and a "10" score would indicate a manager that allows freedom for employees to make decisions freely. In most cases, employees will score the relationship on the lower end and the manager will rate themselves on the higher end. That gap that exists helps to illuminate the autonomy (or lack of it) within the team.

This focus on increased autonomy and control is perhaps the most important of all the options, because at its core, flexibility for any job is about choice. In those jobs that are remote-friendly, it's about a choice of where to work. But in those jobs that are not remote-friendly, the alternative is to offer them a choice of flexibility in **how** their work gets done to the degree it's possible within the confines of the business operations.

It's worth noting in our research on frontline workers, we find that men are most likely to say that they define flexibility around this autonomy/choice in their work. [60] Women are more likely than men to define flexibility as "when" they work, which is a great transition to point number two below.

2) Time off and scheduling options

Offering more granular time off or more flexibility in scheduling seems simple to those of us that don't need it. In many organizations, shifts are determined by managers, and employees have little say in what shift they get assigned. They may also not be allowed to swap shifts without jumping through hoops to make it happen.

The more flexible choice? Allow people to swap shifts. Put the power in their hands. Not only does this give them a bit more control over their work, but it also can take some of the stress off of managers to find workers at the last minute.

On a related note, when it comes to time: consider more granular time flexibility options. A friend works for a local auto manufacturer, and if he needs to see a doctor sometime during the workday, he gets a sort of warning for taking time off. The sense he gets as an employee is that he should have just taken off a whole day to avoid that unpleasant experience. A better practice would be to allow him (or any employee) to use portions of their paid time balance as needed during the day. That could be just an hour if that kind of personal errand was near the workplace.

We see in our research that one of the biggest reasons people don't use time off is because they aren't sure how they are going to be perceived by the business leadership. This is especially true for women in the data. If we're truly offering it as a flexible benefit to help meet their needs, we need to make sure we're treating it as such when it's actually utilized.

3) Progress and mobility options

To continue this conversation, let's give some control to the people over their career progress and growth opportunities.

In our research on Performance, Engagement, and Business Impact, we found that one of the top practices of companies with better revenue, employee retention, and employee engagement scores was weaving growth and development into the performance/talent management process. We're currently in the process of updating this research, and I fully expect to see an even stronger correlation than the last time we measured.

On a more human level, the data indicate that for every employee that is ambivalent about their career growth, there are two employees that crave and desire it. To take it even further, we see that when an employee quits a job because of a lack of career growth, they place an even higher burden on themselves, their manager, and HR/training teams at future jobs because they don't want to be stuck in a dead-end job again.

The way I typically phrase this is helping to "cast a vision" for their future. If managers are not helping to cast a vision for what's next at the company and how they see their people playing a part in that, then those workers will have a vision at another company when they get called by a headhunter or recruiter. We must make this a priority. The perception is most companies is that people have to leave the organization in order to advance their career.

Chipotle is a great example of doing this well. Several years ago, the quick service restaurant chain had tremendous turnover rates in its hourly and salaried managers. For those of you that haven't worked in that industry, these managers are critical. They set work schedules, handle training, order inventory, support customer service, and so much more. So, Chipotle leadership changed one hiring decision around these positions that dramatically dropped turnover overnight: they told leaders they were no longer allowed to hire these managers from outside the ranks of current employees. That's right, no going over to another restaurant competitor and luring their manager away. Instead, they had to select people from existing staff and develop them up into leadership roles.

And if that sounds too good to be true, they don't just leave this to chance. Executives that develop other leaders to take those roles are given an incentive bonus. On top of that, Chipotle has joined other organizations with large hourly workforces in recent years to offer education to its entire team through a third-party partnership with Guild Education. This partnership helps to develop workers for future career opportunities they may want to pursue by expanding the impact and options available under the firm's legacy tuition reimbursement program.

Job applicants told us in a recent study that they prefer a hiring process that evaluates them not just for what they can do **today**, but what their potential is for the **future**. In the long run, what do you think an employee is going to appreciate more: an opportunity to work in a home office for a period of time or an opportunity to leverage their strengths, step into a dream career, and show off the real potential they have?

4) Communication and clarity options

It's a basic human desire to understand what is happening and feel like we have an awareness of what's next. When you work for a leader or a company that is very secretive and unwilling to share information, it can make you feel uncomfortable and unprepared for what's next. That's why being very clear is a key opportunity to provide a sense of flexibility to the workforce. In our 2022

Lighthouse Research & Advisory Frontline Worker Trends study, we found that there was a tight connection between a worker's sense of openness/transparency and their intent to quit their job. Employees that said their employer is not transparent were nearly **four times** more likely to have plans to quit their job.[61]

In the book *The Idea Driven Organization*, the authors talk much about the importance of listening to your people, because innovation primarily comes from those closest to the delivery of the product or service. We want to think that innovation comes from a board room or a remote executive office, but that's uncommon. Most often it comes from the people on the front lines that see a way to improve customer satisfaction by 5% or speed up a process by 10%. Those small increments drive serious value over time as they accumulate. You've seen elsewhere in this book that the entrepreneurial spirit is a powerful thing if harnessed appropriately, and this is one way to create an outlet for those energies and ideas.

Beyond the innovation component, simply being open and clear with the workforce can work wonders. We surveyed 1,000 employees in our Reskilling, Mobility, and Talent Development study in 2022. We found that six out of 10 of them say they do not get any guidance from their leaders on what skills are most important to develop for long-term career success. How can we expect the workforce to be engaged and effective if they feel like they are trying to figure everything out for themselves? In contrast, about 70% of the employers in our study said that they expect managers to flow down skill requirements to their people for development priorities. That's a clear mismatch between expectation and reality.

Be clear. Communicate often. Just because you can't offer someone the option to work from another location doesn't mean you need to shy away from communicating with them overall. Sharing information and requesting input creates a powerful dialogue, one that is based on trust, transparency, and open communications. Not only is communication worth its own focus, but it is also an enabler of some of the policies and approaches outlined in the other flexibility suggestions above.

Finally, a somewhat radical approach to this problem is job redesign. One expert in frontline workplaces shared with me that one of his clients was actually allowing some of its frontline staff to work as customer service professionals for a certain number of hours weekly, creating a sort of hybrid job where they are present in the workplace for a period of time and able to work remotely from home another portion of the time.

This approach is novel and unique. It's also likely difficult to administer. Each of those people need the resources to handle calls from home, including both the technical resources as well as an actual quiet physical space to perform the work. But when it works, it unlocks a different kind of opportunity that most frontline workers never have access to. By redesigning any job and restructuring how it is accomplished, we can trim out those highly repetitive aspects and prioritize focus on the more creative or human-centered ones.

Employee Development, Career Pathing, and Growth

Employees are people. That shouldn't be a newsflash to you, but to some of the people that work at your organization, that may be something they have forgotten over time. Yet we don't often have nearly as much insight into our people as we do other areas of the business. And I'm talking about other non-revenue generating areas of the business, for comparison's sake. Take Property. In large companies, the Property department can tell you where each chair is, what they paid for them, how much they are depreciated, how to find repair parts, and more. But when it comes to our people, we don't always know what they can do, their entire pay history, or what motivates them.

Our people aren't static assets like office chairs. They are an investment that increases in value and appreciates over time, and more importantly they have a free will. If we're not helping them to be more valuable tomorrow than they are today, then that may be a failure on our part, and they will eventually choose to seek out another employer that will meet and fulfill their needs.

In our 2021 research on learning and employee development, two out of three workers admitted to quitting a job at some point in their career because of a lack of growth and development opportunities. Statistically, if you lined up any three of your employees in front of you right now, two of them will fit in this category of quitting due to a lack of growth. But there were two other related findings that speak volumes. First, 90% of those who had quit said they would have considered staying if they saw opportunities available, which means this isn't a permanent problem if we will take steps to address it. Secondly, those people who had quit due to a lack of development placed a higher burden of career development on themselves, their managers, and the HR/training team at subsequent jobs. In other words, after we've quit because of a lack of growth, we don't want to do it again, so we put more pressure on every participant (ourselves, our leaders, and the training team) to make sure it doesn't happen again.

One more data point to add to this list comes from our 2022 Talent Acquisition Trends study. We found that more than 80% of candidates want to learn about career growth opportunities during the hiring process.[62] During a time of intense competition for talent, workers want to know that they have options ahead of them and not just another dead-end job.

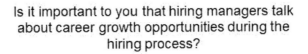

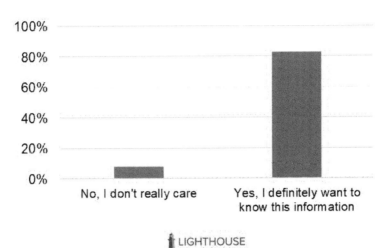

Figure 6.2

But this growth is possible. From simple things like offering development and online training opportunities to more extensive career growth plans, this isn't a pipe dream. When I speak about supporting employees and their career choices, I talk about companies like:

- Chipotle, which hires store managers from internal/existing staff because they are less likely to quit than external hires. The casual restaurant chain even pays managers a bonus if they develop someone into a new leadership role to help incentivize that behavior.
- Social media technology company Hootsuite has a stretch assignment program that allows workers to explore other career options within the business one day a week for a 90-day period. The manager that "borrows" the employee sets expectations on how they will contribute during that time, and the "lending" manager also sets expectations on how the employee will bring back perspectives and value

from the assignment, ensuring that every stretch assignment benefits all stakeholders.

- Bechtel, a government contracting firm with 50,000+ employees in 50 countries, uses mobility assignments as a way to woo and entice high-value candidates and employees to join or stay with the company. A friend who worked there in HR reported up to an HR director who started out as a chemical engineer!

- Credit Suisse uses a simple, yet effective, approach that it calls Internals First. When the company is hiring for a new position, it simply puts existing employees at the front of the line, giving them a chance to consider the opportunity before opening it up externally. The results for the company have been impressive. Nearly 10% of the workforce transitioned internally one year, 39% of all vacancies are filled internally, and at one point, the company was able to fill nearly half of its director-level roles with existing staff.

Or what about Tata Consultancy Services? One of the ways that TCS approaches this is with a very simple interaction between every manager and employee. At the Indian multinational consulting firm with more than 600,000 global staff, managers are taught to ask their team members how they can help them grow and advance. The company places a premium on this upward mobility: its current CEO started with the company as an intern/trainee in 1987. While that same path isn't available for every single employee, it serves as a visible reminder that growth is key, and if we're not growing our people, they are stagnating.

One additional item that seems relevant here: COVID and the time period surrounding it were difficult on everyone. In a time when life was upside down for many people, they were looking for anything they could to cling to for a sense of control over their future. In our 2021 learning study, workers who told us that they had the right kinds of training and growth opportunities available through their company were more than twice as likely to say that their employer helped them adapt to the pandemic and any related workplace changes. It's easy for business leaders like us to see learning and training as just another course or piece of content, but truthfully, it's more than that. People see development as a path for their future. When they have options and opportunities, they don't just feel more in control of their career—they feel more in control of their life.

Hiring and Staffing an Employee-Centric Organization

It's never polite to say, "I told you so," but I've found that you can say it occasionally and get away with it if there's a positive lesson to be learned. For those of us working in the People space, we've said for years that investing in HR staff, programs, and technology can help to drive employee engagement and satisfaction. In 2021 and 2022 when employers were hiring as fast as they possibly could to keep up with demand, the number of job postings for human resources and recruiting professionals went through the roof. The change in demand compared to the baseline was the typical hockey stick growth curve, approximately 600% higher than what economists expected. It's going to be no surprise to any of you here, but suddenly companies were realizing, "Hey, HR takes care of people. If we have enough of these professionals on staff, we can take care of our people and maybe they won't leave." Company leaders are starting to realize that maybe that thing my peers and I have been saying all along really is true.

From a practical perspective, Jane Jaxon, currently the Chief People Officer for Wistia, once told me that the company she was working for at the time had a ratio of one HR staff member per 25 employees. By comparison, the common ratio most often cited in industry publications and resources is one HR staff member to 100 workers, which meant she worked at a company that was investing in HR hiring at four times the normal rate. This high concentration of People team members was due to a highly competitive market (tech company in the Northeastern United States). The company was highly successful in hiring and keeping talent that was being approached daily by competitors looking for a way to hire them away, and it accomplished this by investing in its HR team.

When I think about this mindset transition to prioritize people and HR, the "People people," I think about thermometers. The very first job I ever had where I got to touch on some of the typical human resources tasks among accounting, admin, and other work was at a company that built these large, complex machines. It was incredibly neat, because I don't have any technical ability at all, but I highly respect those people that do. These engineers were building massive machines, and one of them had a use that all of us are probably familiar with.

If you've ever been to a doctor or a hospital and they had those little red boxes or bags of biohazard materials, that's why this machine was being built. You can't put those biohazard materials in the trash, because they are dangerous, so this company operated machines that destroyed those in a way that they weren't dangerous anymore. The machine would sanitize and pressurize it, leaving behind a little lump of inert metal that came out at the end.

As they were building this machine, I received one of these invoices that came in from our vendor that said we purchased two different thermometers: one was $20, and the other was $2,000. My immediate thought is that someone had made a mistake, so I went and talked to our head engineer, and he said that the invoice was correct. Seeing the puzzled look on my face, he quickly explained that the $2,000 thermometer went inside the machine. It notifies the operator when that lump of material has hit that proper temperature to have killed any sort of bacteria or germs or anything else, indicating it is safe. The $20 thermometer is for checking the item's temperature just before an employee picks it up in their hands to make sure it is safe.

This process is how I feel many companies have operated and invested from a People perspective through the years. We're going to spend $2,000 on the business process, but when it comes to the workforce, we're going to skimp and buy the cheapest possible equipment.

That mindset is starting to show up in the data. In our Great Reprioritization study of thousands of North American workers, we found some compelling indicators of why people are planning to quit their jobs and what we can do to keep them. For starters, one in four employees were thinking seriously about quitting their job in the near term. If you lined up four of your random people right now in front of you and you grabbed one of them, one of those people is planning on leaving at some point in the near future. For those people who are thinking about leaving, we started diving into the findings to say, what can we do to keep them? Is it possible, or is it a foregone conclusion that they're gone and there's nothing we can do.

When we examined responses for people who already quit their jobs, we dug into things like what forced them to leave or what drove them away from the company or job. The number one thing overall was stress and burnout. People have been saying there's been so much change and so many things they didn't expect. All of those have piled up and they are leaving to reset their life and reassert a sense of control over things. When we look at frontline workers specifically, their biggest reason for leaving was seeking out higher pay, which was the second highest response for the workforce overall. The last of the top three reasons for quitting was because the worker didn't like the company's policies, leadership, or culture. That's pretty broad, but it allows us to see that the **top two reasons for leaving a job were very individualized in nature**.

But that's not the end of this discussion. Remember in preschool or kindergarten where you'd have to draw a line across the page to match things up? We can do that same thing with this research, connecting the reasons people leave with the things they say would make them stay in a job. Let's see that top list of reasons for quitting again:

1. Stress and burnout
2. Better pay/benefits
3. Company policy/leadership/culture

Now, let's bring in the top three things that works said would make them stay in a job:

1. Better pay/benefits
2. Better work/life balance
3. More flexibility options

You can probably do this yourself, but I'll make it easy by connecting the dots below between the quit reasons and the retention preferences:

Reason for Quitting	What Makes a Worker Stay
1) Stress and burnout	Better work/life balance, more flexibility options
2) Seeking better pay/benefits	Better pay and benefits, more flexibility in benefit options
3) Company policy, leadership, and culture	Better work/life balance, more flexibility options

This is a bit oversimplified, but I share it because we see that in many cases, people don't have to or want to quit jobs where they are having their needs met. Most of the time quitting is a last resort when an employee feels like nothing in their employment situation can change for the better. The psychologist Henry Cloud wrote in his book *Necessary Endings* about the fact that when we lose hope in any relationship, be it work or personal, it's time to end that relationship for our own good. While people leave work for plenty of other reasons, the data we have indicate that those top reasons were preventable as we've discussed here.

Moving on, I believe we as business and talent leaders want to do the right thing for our staff. I'm firmly convinced of that based on hundreds of research interviews with incredible voices throughout our space as well as events like HR Summer School, a virtual series I've co-led since 2020 that has reached more than 10,000 HR leaders with a combination of education and inspiration. I hear from these People practitioners that they are constantly learning, growing, and stretching in order to serve their organization and workforce in a better way. Across the board, most of us are spending a lot of time trying to figure out what's the next right thing we can do to support and keep our people. And not just to keep them around, but to keep them engaged and productive. It's not easy, and part of that difficulty is because the expectations of the workforce have changed over time. Consider the following example from our research.

If you accepted a job offer, how long would you consider other jobs? How long would you entertain other conversations about other positions and openings? In our Great Reprioritization study, we asked this question to the workforce, and you can see the responses on the next page.

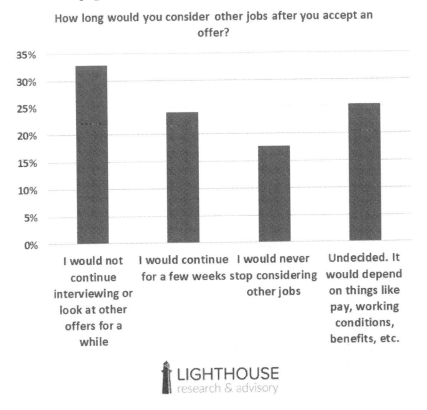

Figure 6.3[63]

This response surprised me on multiple levels. For starters, just one in three workers say they would stop considering other jobs after they accept a job offer. That feels like a real shift in what is socially acceptable, because when I accepted jobs in the past, I didn't keep searching and looking for something else. That acceptance was a commitment.

The other finding that surprised me in this was that women were much more likely than men to respond on the far right, saying they would always be open to the right offer. I incorrectly assumed than men would want that freedom of not being tied down or held back. As I was examining the findings from this study, I had a chance recently to speak with an HR executive who has had a tremendous and amazing career. She's been just a great resource over the years, so I asked for her input on this. Her response was straightforward, "Yep, that's obvious." Seeing the look on my face, she explained further that she had worked in too many jobs throughout her career where she wasn't respected, and her voice didn't matter. In short, she was made to feel like she wasn't heard. So, if an employer approaches her, and they respect her for who she is and what she stands for, she will **always** entertain those conversations, because she has been in too many jobs and too many companies where they did not respect that. Her comments on that completely changed my perspective here and made tremendous sense. The moral of the story: employers that want to gain more commitment from the women they are recruiting (or retaining) must ensure that their voices are heard, celebrated, and elevated, or they will find another employer that will.

While we're talking about differences in perspective, let's look at age groups in the workplace. The way we see and experience work at 25 is very different than how we experience it at age 55, and what we seek from work evolves as we change, mature, and grow. When we ask workers what their top priorities are at work, we see those items we discussed above: work/life balance, flexibility, and pay/benefits. But when we break that out by age group, something interesting happens. Take a look at the following for a moment before you read further. When you compare each age group, can you see what is unique about the responses?

Age Bracket	Priority #1	Priority #2
18-24	Work/life balance	Relationships
25-34	Work/life balance	Compensation
35-44	Work/life balance	Career growth
45-54	Compensation	Relationships
54+	Compensation	Benefits

Age/Stage Priorities

Figure 6.4

Did you see it?

When we look at any age group in relation to another, **there's not a single pair of them with the same top two priorities**. From a practical perspective, it reiterates a point made earlier, which is the fact that it's very difficult to create an approach that meets the needs of every single person in the workplace. We're all too different for a one size fits all approach.

Taking everything into account from the last few pages, answer this question for me: does this look like employees saying "I'm out of here. I'm quitting and there's nothing you can do about it." Or are they saying, "I would consider staying if you'd make some changes or address my work preferences." Hopefully you come to the same conclusion that I did, which is the latter.

Despite all the headlines saying people were quitting work during the "Great Resignation" for no particular reason, this survey was taken during the middle of that time period. Clearly, we see here that the people who have their concerns addressed have little to no interest in quitting their jobs, while at the same time those who don't have those needs addressed are planning to quit their jobs in the near future.

The Most Critical Factor in Employee Retention

Did you know that we could do one thing that would change employee retention for the better and dramatically improve that metric? That one thing is the most important relationship any of us has in the workplace, and the research shows an incredible connection between that relationship and workplace satisfaction, productivity, retention rate, and so much more. In fact, this relationship has been shown in some research to make up as much as 70% of someone's satisfaction on the job.[64] You might have already guessed it, but the relationship I'm talking about is the one between an employee and their direct manager.

In the book *All In*, authors Chester Elton and Adrian Gostick point out a study that attempted to understand the variations between high-performing and low-performing teams in an organization.[65] The company wondered if it was due to any number of variables, from the number of superstars on the team to tools and technology and everything in between. In one of their experiments, the company took the managers of those teams that were green, or performing above average, and they put them in teams that were red (performing below average). Then they sat back, and they watched for three months. When they came back and measured, they found something incredible.

What they saw was the green teams that received a red manager were suddenly performing in the red three months later. Not just one person, but the entire team's performance. It was below average, even though it had the same tools and the same people as before. And the inverse was also true: where they put a green manager, those teams ended up performing above average, which radically changed everything they thought they knew about teamwork in the business.

This is one small example of just how much managers matter. In our findings, we saw that if someone says "my manager doesn't support me," that person wasn't just more likely to leave at some vague point far into the future, but **within the next 30 days**.

Many of us have probably worked for leaders like that in the past. I know that I have. In those situations, you can tell they don't care, and from the employee perspective, there's absolutely nothing wrong with saying, "If you don't care, why should I care? I'll find somewhere else to work and someone that will care about me." This is what we call the **efficacy of care**. In medical terms, the efficacy of a treatment tells us how effective it is at treating a disease or injury. In this case, efficacy is about understanding what a manager can do to care for and support their people, because the results of that are astounding.

Let me tell you about a real-life example of this to show it's possible and also to give you an idea of what it looks like from a practical, everyday perspective.

Years ago, in my first HR job after college, I was working for a nonprofit organization that provided direct care to mentally ill individuals as well as those with disabilities. I had the envious position of having the least seniority, so my work was pretty basic: managing all the employee files. Every piece of paper that was created in the entire organization's 600-plus employees went across my desk at some point. The majority of my work was processing new hires and processing terminations. See, we had turnover of 50-plus percent a year, which was overwhelming when you think about the number of people we were hiring only to fill their positions again not long after. In fact, some days I had the new hire and termination paperwork for the same person arrive on the same day to process! During my interview, I remember them telling me that we had 50% turnover, and it was a known problem that had yet to be addressed in any way I could see.

Even as the new guy on the team, I wondered what the limit could be to this seemingly untenable treadmill of hiring activity we were on. At some point we had to run out of people to hire, right? So, I took it upon myself to start cataloguing our employee data from the previous years into our new HR system. It was little more than a spreadsheet, but it at least made the data visible so I could see if there were any trends to examine. I pulled in all kinds of figures, from the tenure to the location to the manager.

As I was analyzing this information, I realized something interesting. While the 50% turnover was the average across the organization, it changed based on location and manager. We had one manager with 70-80% turnover and another with 10 to 20%. In general, all of these people were doing the exact same work for the same pay rate, so that didn't make sense to me. These individuals were providing direct care for clients with developmental or intellectual disabilities, and the work was stressful, challenging, and draining. There were 24-hour shifts. The pay was very low for us as a nonprofit organization. So why the big gap in turnover figures across the organization?

In order to hopefully learn some valuable lessons, I went in and sat down with Antione, the leader of the area with the lowest turnover. I wanted to shadow him and see what was happening to try to find out what practices I could replicate across the business. That morning, Antoine had a new hire starting her job. What I saw next showed me the secret of reducing turnover, increasing employee satisfaction, and creating a team that outperforms all others.

The young lady sat down in Antoine's office, and he smiled brightly and handed her a letter, saying, "I have some details here for you, because I know you'll have a lot of things come at you on your first day. I just want to take a moment and tell you that I'm really, really excited to have you on my team. I know you're going to do great things here, and our clients are blessed to have you working with them. I know you will have questions and challenges in your time here, and I want you to know my door is open. More importantly, I want you to know that **I** am open to whatever you need. I can't wait to see you grow, succeed, and make an impact on the lives of others. Welcome!"

Can I tell you that I briefly thought about quitting my job in HR and going to work with Antoine because he was so encouraging and so inspiring as a leader? I was amazed, because I had never worked for anyone who treated me that way, and I'm willing to bet that this person taking this job for $7.50 an hour had never had anyone treat her that way either. I love to tell this story about Antoine for a few reasons. First, because this is a tremendous reminder that these leaders exist. They are everywhere. Every business has someone like Antoine, and it's someone that is drawn to serving others through leadership. It is our job to find those people and celebrate their stories so others can learn from them. Secondly, I tell this story because it's my reminder that all jobs and people are worthy. It's not just someone in a "professional" role. Even when I worked in "professional" jobs, nobody had ever treated me as well as Antoine treated this young woman.

I am really diving in here on managers and how they lead their people because all of the things we've covered so far are jointly owned and delivered to our people. What I mean by that is we as a leadership or HR team may say that we believe in work/life balance, but that's going to work or fall apart at the level of that manager's interaction with their people. Unfortunately, we have come to believe that things like workplace flexibility, a focus on an inclusive culture, or even work/life balance are simple policy decisions. Yes, there can be a policy element to any of these things, but they exist at a **relationship** level. That manager's relationship with their people will make those policies work or make them fall apart.

Not only that, but these managers have to be partners for us. In this book you will find ideas, concepts, and strategies to hire and keep people. But you can't do it alone, no matter how large your People team. You need your managers to be successful. I look at our managers as partners in this. If we can get our managers moving in the right direction, that's a high-leverage activity. From a practical perspective, let's look at some of what the research shows can be effective from a manager standpoint.

First of all, I have to believe that people in managerial roles don't wake up in the morning asking, "How can I be as mediocre as possible at leading others today?" Instead, they often want to do well, but they aren't sure how. Or they don't have the right tools. Or they don't have the right training. Every leader is different, and some are motivated and encouraged by data while others are motivated and encouraged by relationships and other aspects of work. If you have the managers that are a little more analytical, feel free to use the data I'm sharing with you. If you have managers that are more relational, these points should resonate with them and lead to better relationships as well. Let's dive in.

We did a study on performance practices a few years back, examining 250 different companies and how they run their performance management processes. There were some incredible findings, but one of the top five things that high-performing employers (those with better revenue, retention, and employee engagement scores) do differently is focus on the strengths of the individual person. They don't treat them like checker pieces, where they're all interchangeable and they're all the same. Can you imagine if all of your people had the same mood, the same strengths, and the same weaknesses? Instead, they treat them like chess pieces where each has their unique focus, their unique strengths, and their unique gifts. Great managers focus on those.

Another of the top things those companies do differently is weaving recognition into how they support and enable worker performance every day. Just like Antoine's example where he recognized the value of the person and what they had to offer, this can be incredibly powerful. Recognition isn't just a random, momentary pat on the back. It's about giving kudos to a specific behavior and encouraging that behavior in the future

Lastly, one of the things that we see is highly correlated with employee support is meeting regularly. In fact, the inverse of this was also true. When we look at the data, a low-performing company has more managers that meet with their people infrequently. So frequency on how often they get together is important. And I know you might be saying, "One-on-ones? Yeah, okay. I get it." But this incredibly simple practice is underestimated so often.

Recently I talked to Guardant Health, a life sciences organization, and published an amazing case study about them and what they're doing, because they have a unique approach to this. They have started using one-on-ones as a targeted way to reduce the likelihood of someone leaving their job.[66] This wasn't just about giving managers more to do. Their HR team understand that managers are really overworked. They're trying to be a coach and a player. They're trying to contribute and do subject matter expert work. They're also trying to manage a team and it's hard for them to balance all those things. So Guardant Health is using some tools on the retention side to support managers by highlighting people who haven't had one-on-ones in a certain period of time, because they see retention risk climb when that time period elapses.

If you work for one of those companies that has tried this, but it didn't stick, here are some real numbers for you: I compared the cost of a 30-minute one-on-one with that manager and their direct report using the median wage in the U.S. ($71,456) and an average manager salary of $100,000. Then I also calculated the cost of losing one person.

- The cost of a 30-minute one-on-one meeting between the manager and their employee for an entire year: $2,160
- The cost of losing that same employee: up to $35,000
- The cost of losing a $10/hour employee, by comparison: $4,000+

Think on that for a moment. Managers push back on investing time in one-on-one meetings because it's not like their employees are verbally identifying a lack of attention as the reason they are going to leave. But even if they did this, it would still cost less than losing that person. Every day managers are trading $4,000+ for $2,160. We can say they are doing it unknowingly, but it doesn't change the result.

There's an old joke about a man who buys coconuts at five cents and sells them for two cents and ends up with a million dollars. How did he do it? He started with two million dollars. That same silly, unrealistic scenario that makes us shake our head with disbelief (surely nobody would really do that, would they?) is exactly what is happening every day in our organizations as leaders fail to meet regularly with their people, **dramatically** increasing their chances of quitting.

In early 2022, when employers were struggling to find recruiters and keep them on staff, I spoke with the leader of a recruiting company. In her words, recruiters were the lifeblood of her organization. Without recruiters, the revenue would dry up and the company would cease to exist. But she mentioned that she hadn't lost a single recruiter yet to competing firms. Knowing the incredibly intense pressure to hire and keep recruiting talent, I asked her for her secret.

Her not-so-secret secret was spending time with each of the recruiters on an individual basis. Even though they were remote, she had dedicated a significant portion of every week to talking one-on-one with each of them to discuss their challenges, understand their needs, or just commiserate on the difficulties of hiring in a tight talent market. Bottom line: this is a powerful practice, and this is a great example of how it can help to maintain stability and retention even in the midst of outrageous job offers above market rates.

The Complicated Relationship Between
Managers and Employee Turnover Data

Imagine that you have a new job. You are responsible for reporting on leaks in a dam. I'll note that:

- You don't have any of the tools to fix the dam. Marcus has those.

- You have no oversight of the repair schedule or practices. That's Isha's job.

- You can't control who damages the dam by driving recklessly, even though Sally has wrecked into it twice just this month.

You just show up in meetings and report on the leaks. Over and over, you share data on these numbers, and you try to soften the blow by giving reasons or excuses, because none of the other three people are present in the meeting to explain their actions.

If you haven't figured it out yet, I'm sharing this example to help us visualize employee turnover through another lens. Month after month across the globe, HR and talent leaders share data about how many employees left the company, even though the vast majority of turnover reasons have to do with their relationship with their direct manager. We try to explain away turnover, but unless that turnover happens within our own teams, we really can't make any decisions that measurably change how it plays out.

One of the lines of thinking I have appreciated over the last few years is that managers should have more responsibility for reporting their own turnover numbers. It may be farfetched, but letting those individuals sit on the "hot seat" while explaining why that high-performing team member left would be fairer, and anyone unhappy about losing that person could direct their ire at the person most responsible for the departure.

From a practical perspective, as manager enablement expert Kamaria Scott puts it, managers don't need to know what engagement is, they need to know **how** to be engaging.[67] They need to know that retention is a key measure of a successful team. They need to know that their performance as a leader is just as important as their performance as a contributor, for those that have both sets of responsibilities.

Again, I lean towards practical tools, and one that Ms. Scott recommends is, in simple terms, a manager circle. All too often we select managers based on tenure or other factors that aren't relevant to their ability to lead a team. And once selected for a leadership role, we find that it's hard for managers to raise their hands to ask for help. Manager circles are essentially made up of a cohort of new leaders that meet to support and encourage each other. Maybe a manager has to discipline someone for the first time or needs ideas on how to motivate a team member. Whatever the case, they can bring it up in the manager circle because it's a safe space for idea sharing and collaborating on solutions.

Or what about allowing managers to "try before they buy" by experimenting in the role first? In an interview with Pat Wadors, a former talent executive at LinkedIn and Yahoo, she explained an experiment at one of her previous employers where individual contributors were given a chance to test drive a leadership role for a period of time before they had to fully commit to the position.

> *We experimented and said, let's have a trial run at being a manager. We took about 25 people that wanted to be a manager as a cohort. We said, okay, for a period of six to nine months, we would give you a small team you'd be responsible to learn how to interview and make hiring decisions. Then you get to decide whether or not you want to continue the manager path or not.*[68]

How revolutionary is that decision? We know from our research that employees who work for a manager that doesn't support them are twice as likely to quit their job in the next 30 days. If we use methods like this to help pick better leaders, we may be able to dramatically reduce the number of people who quit their jobs because they don't feel like their manager supports them.

Here's a final example from a world leader in healthcare: the Mayo Clinic. In a discussion with one of their subject matter experts in talent science and leadership selection, I learned that they don't pick leaders based solely on their ideas, their performance, or their charisma. They pick leaders based on how well they inspire and elevate the performance of those around them.[69] They realize that the cost of a poor leader is nearly incalculable as we think about the damage they can do to team performance, culture, and customer (or patient) satisfaction. But the value of a great leader is also hard to determine, because there are so many direct and indirect benefits of having someone in a role where they support and inspire the best from their people every day.

If only we could snap our fingers and make this all work, right? The relationship between managers and People teams has always been a bit of a stressful one, but that doesn't have to be true perpetually. One of my mentors is a marriage counselor, and he says that relationships can change dramatically when both participants decide to stop fighting **about** something and start fighting **for** something together. This is true for HR and the managers within the business.

As I've already pointed out, there are numerous policy decisions we can make, but they often scale down to relationship decisions between people at work. Let's find ways to fight together to keep our people. Let's find ways to work together to create a workplace that others envy. Let's find ways to elevate our employee experience so that people don't just like coming to work, but they also love inviting other high performers to join the company as well. That's what success looks like in my opinion, and the research reflects that. In our 2022 Frontline Worker Trends study of thousands of global frontline staff, workers who had a manager they claimed was supportive were many times more likely to say they would recommend the company as a great place to work to their friends.

From a more theoretical perspective, we all learned in Psychology 101 that when our brains are faced with danger, we turn to fight or flight. That's true in a sense of physical danger, but it's also true in terms of psychological danger as well.[70] Most employees operate at work under an "all systems safe" mentality, which means they are able to work and focus without being concerned for their safety. However, that's not the highest order of functioning.

Our brains are hardwired to look for danger. It's a built-in protection from ancient days where there might be a tiger or lion hiding behind the next tree. Even in modern times when we logically know the chances of that happening are so low that the probability is essentially zero, we still worry with some part of our brain. In the workplace, we worry less about wildlife and more about how our ideas are received, whether we'll get recognized for that effort we put in, or how secure our job might be. But when we're in a place where we feel like we belong and are safe, we unlock that last bit of creativity, effort, and focus that we've been holding back and can put it into our work relationships, tasks, and ideas.

This is more than just a hypothesis. The evidence shows that when we feel like we truly are **accepted, respected,** and **appreciated** (which is the psychological definition of belonging) we respond differently than the average person in a variety of situations.[71] In fact, some of our new research insights on this are pretty compelling.

- **Frontline worker study**: High Belonging frontline workers are 2.5x less likely to have plans to quit their job, 1.75x more likely to say they are paid fairly, and 5x more likely to recommend their employer as a great place to work.

- **Learning and career development study**: Low Belonging employees are 8x more likely to say that no learning is interesting to them and 6x more likely to say they think their company is headed in a negative direction.

- **Workplace wellbeing study**: High Belonging staff are 2.7x more likely to say their employer made positive changes to support health and wellbeing, and they are also 44% less likely to have thought about quitting their job due to mental health and stress. Most importantly, they are 16x more likely to say their company has a strong culture of health and wellbeing.

A great comparison on High and Low Belonging sentiment from our 2022 Mental Health and Wellbeing Trends study is included below.

PLEASE RATE YOUR PERSONAL MENTAL HEALTH

	HIGH BELONGING	LOW BELONGING
EXCELLENT	31%	8%
VERY GOOD	38%	19%
GOOD	29%	36%
FAIR	9%	25%
POOR	1%	12%

Figure 6.5

All of this discussion around belonging is to reiterate again just how important it is that someone feels connected and supported at work. This can't just be an HR or talent issue. We have to have managers serving as that critical connection point if we want our workforce to feel like they are in the right job at the right company.

One of the phrases that has become commonplace in recent years is "bring your best self to work." Like this discussion on belonging, that can feel very soft and intangible. But I believe these two concepts are highly related. When we have people who are respected, accepted, and appreciated at work, they can truly bring their very best effort and ideas to the table. They can lean in to finish that project before the deadline. They can pick up the slack when a coworker is out sick. They can do all of those very tangible things, but they will only do them if they feel like they have real worth and value.

But what if our employees ask for something we can't give them?

This question comes up in every webinar or speaking event where I've talked about the importance of surveys and employee listening programs. We as a community of People leaders are simply terrified that employees will ask for something that's outside of our ability to deliver and that they will suddenly be angry because we can't meet their needs. I will say that there's an element to this that **is** important, and that's acknowledgement. If someone asks for pie and we give them cake without an explanation, they will likely feel like they wasted their time telling us what they want. But if we can't give them pie because of reasons X, Y, or Z, then we should let them know why cake is the best option we're able to provide within our budget and other constraints.

Acknowledge their request, regardless of whether you can meet it or not. I saw this play out firsthand in one of my early jobs as an HR generalist. We picked up a couple dozen new employees when we won a new contract, but none of them were staff that we had screened and hired with our normal process. When our team went to visit them for the first time, their collective attitude was skeptical at best and jaded at worst. So, our team put together a list of the top complaints from the team and began to systematically work down the list. When I revisited them, I was able to show them the list of issues based on their inputs and which ones we 1) had already addressed 2) were planning to address and 3) could not address for various reasons. I can't tell you how that single interaction changed the tenor of those relationships, leading to friendships I still appreciate today more than a dozen years later.

Every single one of our employees carries some of that same baggage. They had a manager who didn't appreciate them or a company that was a black hole of information where nothing was shared openly. It's up to us to show them that isn't the only way that the employment relationship exists.

Within the scope of this chapter, we've covered some interesting an important ground. I'd like to say that there's a new method that we just discovered engaged and unlikely to leave our companies, but the truth is that just isn't the case.

- Managers who care about their people have always been a key contributor of employee growth and retention.
- Opportunities to grow and advance someone's skills and/or career have been useful for keeping people

motivated for a very long time.
- Flexibility that breeds trust and openness has been a currency for as long as humans have interacted with each other in any meaningful capacity.

It's my hope that by sharing the research and other stories that we can start making some of these actions more relatable, practical, and actionable, not just aspirational. In a world where talent scarcity reigns, we can't take employee retention for granted. Every single person we have will be more valuable than ever, and if we don't show them that we realize that, someone else will.

> ## Case Study: How a Trucking Company Retains Record Levels of Drivers in an Industry with a Perpetual Shortage

In an industry with 90+% turnover rates (that's not a typo), anyone who can solve for that will stand out from the crowd. Nussbaum Trucking's employee turnover stands at **less than one-third** of that industry-wide number. And according to the company's Chief Administrative Officer Jeremy Stickling, their "secret" isn't really a secret at all.[72]

Longstanding research shows that people want to feel a sense of progress and advancement, but as Stickling points out, "When you're a driver, your career ladder ends at the steering wheel." Unlike some other professions like plumbers or electricians, drivers don't really have certifications or other levels to distinguish their skills or learning. Nussbaum has created a program it calls CertRed to help drivers grow those skills and become not just more valuable employees, but a more engaged workforce as well. CertRed is voluntary, but it includes online learning, phone counseling, video content, peer to peer interaction, and hands on sessions when on site at corporate.

While this is valuable, there are plenty of companies that offer training and still have high turnover. The real difference is less tangible, yet even more impactful: the company's values. Stickling says that to the leadership at Nussbaum, humans have intrinsic value. They make the business work. They serve the customers. And they aren't "throw away" resources like they seem to be treated at so many other companies. So, yes, even in an industry like trucking where you might expect a tough, gruff workforce to be prevalent, Nussbaum's team isn't afraid to love its people, serve them well, and care for their needs. Stickling actually used a word that is uncommon in the workplace, but it stands out as part of their overall approach, and that's **stewardship**. The company's leadership feels like stewards, or caretakers, for the people who work there. And by extension, the drivers and other workers feel like stewards of the company name, and that sense of ownership is very different than it would be at most other companies.

The results speak for themselves. The company's approval rating from its workforce is 85%, the turnover rate is 29%, and their culture has been recognized by multiple awards as the best company to drive for. In an industry like trucking with a perpetual shortage of drivers, these types of values and actions are how employers will have to stand out if they want to remain viable, competitive, and profitable.

45 https://www.protocol.com/bulletins/tech-recruiter-layoffs-next-steps
46 https://travel.state.gov/content/dam/visas/Statistics/Immigrant-Statistics/WaitingList/WaitingListItem_2020_vF.pdf
47 https://www.dw.com/en/germany-to-introduce-green-card-to-bolster-workforce/a-63046971
48 https://www.hiringlab.org/2022/06/09/fair-chance-hiring-job-ads-rise/
49 https://onlyhumanshow.com/e/hr-s-role-in-driving-organizational-success-with-julie-salomone-on-we-re-only-human/
50 https://onlyhumanshow.com/e/were-only-human-58-open-sourcing-the-recruiting-playbook-from-northwestern-mutual/
51 https://drjohnsullivan.com/articles/complete-guide-boomerang-recruiting/
52 https://enterprisealumni.com/news/corporate-alumni/who-are-alumni/
53 https://www.bls.gov/opub/ted/2021/number-of-people-75-and-older-in-the-labor-force-is-expected-to-grow-96-5-percent-by-2030.htm
54 https://onlyhumanshow.com/e/were-only-human-22-using-referrals-and-purpose-how-allieduniversal-hires-90000-workers-a-year/
55 https://www.nytimes.com/2014/05/15/business/retirementspecial/the-age-premium-retaining-older-workers.html
56 https://finance.yahoo.com/news/budget-airline-aims-lure-empty-133446233.html
57 https://onlyhumanshow.com/e/were-only-human-56-how-delta-airlines-designs-its-candidate-experience/
58 https://positivepsychology.com/hedonic-treadmill/
59 http://www.pnas.org/content/early/2010/08/27/1011492107.abstract
60 https://lhra.io/blog/3-frontline-worker-trends-salary-shortage-and-support/
61 https://lhra.io/blog/what-frontline-workers-want-most-in-2023-infographic/
62 http://lhra.io/ta2022
63 https://lhra.io/blog/data-preview-the-great-resignation-nope-its-the-great-

reprioritization-new-research/

[64] https://news.gallup.com/businessjournal/182792/managers-account-variance-employee-engagement.aspx

[65] https://amzn.to/3lm31aU

[66] https://lhra.io/blog/how-guardant-health-leverages-procaire-by-praisidio-for-employee-retention-case-study/

[67] https://onlyhumanshow.com/e/don-t-teach-managers-about-engagement-teach-them-to-be-engaging/

[68] https://onlyhumanshow.com/e/better-managers-better-support-better-results/

[69] https://onlyhumanshow.com/e/how-mayo-clinic-selects-leaders-a-case-study/

[70] http://respecteffectbook.com/

[71] https://www.tandfonline.com/doi/full/10.1080/02671522.2019.1615116

[72] https://onlyhumanshow.com/e/engaging-a-field-based-workforce-lessons-from-nussbaum-transportation-on-were-only-human/

7

TECHNOLOGY AND AUTOMATION AS GAP FILLERS

In 2020 most of the world stopped hiring, at least for a short while. When companies that operated in public locations began to reopen, they needed to staff up quickly in order to meet deadlines. One theme park had this problem and solved it in a unique way: by hiring 10,000 entry level jobs with no recruiter intervention or hiring manager interviews. Now I'll admit that there was plenty of coordination and planning up front and no shortage of work to do on the back end, but the primary interactions during those hiring activities were handled by job ads, automated assessments, and emails triggered by specific candidate activity. The setup was fairly straightforward:

- Sourcing specialists pushed out communications and advertisements that the company was hiring.
- Applicants applied for jobs and were given an opportunity to complete an assessment closely related to the job duties.
- Successful completion of the assessment triggered a message to self-schedule their visit to the location with their identification documents to prove their eligibility to work.

In just three weeks, 10,000 people were hired and the company was able to train them and open to the public on time. Now, this may generate a variety of feelings with those of us who have done our own screening and recruiting in the past. You may be impressed (I still am). You may be nervous or disbelieving. You may not know how to feel just yet. All of those are perfectly normal, but the truth is that it happened, and this story has been repeated time and time again since then as companies look for ways to streamline hiring and make it more repeatable.

The big part of this story that surprises most people is the automation. It's not quite a "set it and forget it" kind of thing, but in the past, this type of activity would have required dozens of people to make 10,000 hires, and it would have likely taken more than three weeks to accomplish that goal. Automation is a powerful tool, and it can help us in a variety of ways with minimizing busy work and maximizing our time. However, this story might have ended very differently if we were talking about hiring accountants, engineers, or data scientists. When we're bringing in a cashier or a ticket-taker, an automated process is probably satisfactory. At higher skill, pay, and/or responsibility levels, there needs to be a human connection.

In a recent conversation with the team at Advanced RPO, their team said that in some cases, candidates are actually trying to slow down the hiring process slightly in order to get a better feel for the company and its people. While recruiters and companies want to fill jobs as efficiently as possible, candidates want to make sure they are making the right personal and professional decision, and speed isn't the best measurement of that. Not only are they holding up on speed, but they are looking at ways to interact with a human. We still have a desire in many situations and transactions for human interaction. The model I built for my first book shows where those decisions fall on a spectrum.

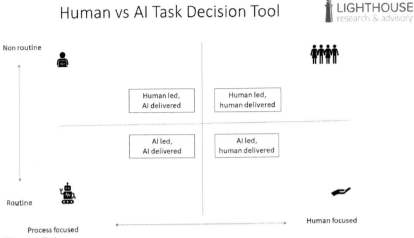

Figure 7.1

Can I tell you a secret? When I was writing my first book *Artificial Intelligence for HR* back in 2017, I was really focused on the technologies, tools, and systems. I was doing my best to bring the stories and examples I had run across in my 300+ conversations with different HR technology vendors every year into the pages of that book. But as I neared the end, I had a concern.

See, I'm very careful to talk about these tools not as a matter of hype, but for the way they help us to focus more on the human activities that really matter. I began to worry that if someone read the book from beginning to end and saw the seemingly endless ways that automation and machine learning were taking apart bits and pieces of the role of HR, talent, and learning professionals, those same practitioners might be worried about the future of this amazing people-focused set of disciplines.

So, I circled back with my publisher to tell them I was adding a final chapter. That chapter, which focuses on the human skills of work, ended up becoming my favorite one of the entire book! Instead of finishing the book and feeling worried or hopeless, anyone that reads that chapter will feel hope for the future, because all of the research points to the fact that automation leaves behind the human aspects of work, and what job is more human-focused than HR?

Every year my team examines dozens of technologies in order to determine and present the HR Tech Awards (HRTechAwards.org) program, where we select some of the world's most impressive technologies across hiring, learning, analytics, workforce, and other categories. Across the board, one key theme that has continued over the last few years is a bigger push towards automating in an intelligent way.

It's no surprise. According to recent data, the number of job postings for human resources professionals is more than 500% higher than economists expected. A wide variety of factors play into this, but the reality is companies are trying to identify and implement different methods, processes, and practices to support their most valuable asset: an engaged workforce. Hiring more HR staff is a good way to do that, but with the technologies getting smarter, we can often leverage them to fill the gap and shift work around in smarter ways.

In one of my first jobs, I had the unenviable task of keeping up with filing and paperwork for all employee-related actions. Tracking and filing paperwork on hiring, promotions, disciplinary actions, and terminations was my daily routine. When I tried to stray from that to do work that I thought might be more valuable, I was quickly pulled back in line by my supervisor.

After two years, I got an offer to move to another company with more meaningful work, better pay, and a supportive manager. My supervisor called a team meeting to decide who would take on my tasks after I left, because the company couldn't afford to add another person at that time. After an hour of discussion and deliberation, it was determined that nobody really needed to do my work.

That's right. **The work I had been doing for two years wasn't really important enough to continue doing.**

It was a strange feeling to be sitting there and thinking back over the prior two years at the work I had done and was proud of, only to realize that it wasn't really adding enough measurable value that the leader thought it should continue. On one hand, I felt justified in the times I had tried to expand the role into other, higher value activities.

On the other, it felt like the 4,000+ working hours of the previous two years were a waste of time I could never get back. When I think about the specific kind of work I was doing, it was not human-focused. It was highly routine and repetitive, generating little measurable value, which is typically a recipe for work that should be automated.

Don't worry, I don't harbor any hard feelings. I get it.

- Not all work necessarily needs to be done.
- And for that work that is necessary, not all of that work needs to be done by a human.
- And of that work that is done by a human, not all of it needs to be done *exclusively* by a human.

Are you following along? Here's another way to look at it: Seth Godin is arguably one of the smartest marketing and business minds of our time. In a recent conversation, a reporter asked him about his thoughts on the future of work. His response fits well here: "Any job I can fully define, I can find someone else to do it cheaper."[73] If I can add to that, I'd add "find someone else **or automate it** to do it cheaper" to round out his comments. Setting any feelings or emotions about this statement aside, it's logically true. If you have a job where you know exactly what task or workflow someone will be doing at any particular point in time, that's a highly structured job. It's easy and inexpensive to outsource or offshore those tasks, and it's becoming increasingly easy and appealing to automate those types of work as well.

When we consider that in the context of what happens in an economic sense, we double down on the likelihood that jobs are going to be consumed by automation. In a 2012 report published by the National Bureau of Economic Research, data indicated that 88% of the routine jobs lost in the United States since the 1980s disappeared within 12 months of an economic downturn. Remember that routine job I held? It disappeared right around the time of the 2008 recession. While the 2020 recession may not have had the same impact because of the unique circumstances associated with it, other recessionary periods will continue to lead to additional automation of jobs previously done by humans.

Automation alone can sometimes feel like a scary concept, but it's going to have to become more of a common discussion at work not just because of the practical implications (fewer workers and the same or greater amount of work to get done, for one) but because of the higher expectation that we have for a personalized and human-centric experience.

When automation happens, the work that gets left behind is more human in nature. In my previous book, *Artificial Intelligence for HR*, I looked at some incredible data that covered automation for the last few hundred years. That includes everything from mechanical improvements over time to digital automation in more recent history. What happens time and time again is automation targets the parts of work that are routine, repetitive, and predictable. Jobs with those traits are more easily automated, and within any specific job, those types of tasks are always good candidates for automation.

As those types of activities are stripped out of any job, what's left behind? This has been a question asked by many, and I won't belabor the point too heavily here other than to highlight what we've found to be the human skills of work.

1. Creativity: the ability to innovate and create new solutions
2. Curiosity: the willingness to ask questions and consider new alternative paths
3. Collaboration: working alongside other people and technologies to solve problems together
4. Critical Thinking: adapting your thinking to new situations and challenges
5. Compassion: prioritizing the human connection whenever possible through care and concern for others

I don't intend to go deeper here, but suffice to say we are going to see this shift in the human skills that we prioritize in hiring and retention long-term. It's happened every time automation has occurred in the past, and it's going to continue to into the future.

The Real Value of Automation Isn't Always Automation, It's What Comes Next

Have you ever been really excited to revisit a favorite restaurant? When you walk in the front door, you can already taste the meal, and your mouth is watering. After you order your food, the server drops off a little basket of bread on the table while you wait. That item, whether it's breadsticks, rolls, or some other similar form, isn't meant to replace your meal. It's not filling in a lasting way. It's not nutritious on a broad scale. And compared to your absolute favorite dish, the taste isn't even on the same level.

Yet we eat it anyway.

Why?

Part of the reason is because we're hungry. Part of the reason is because it's (usually) free. And part of the reason, frankly, is because it's just *there* for the eating. But I'd like to think that none of us would eat that and then decide to skip that favorite dish entirely. That's ludicrous.

I'm leaning heavily on this familiar experience because I want to make a very clear point here: automation is often like that bread. Automation serves a purpose (or multiple purposes), but it isn't meant to entirely replace the primary activity. It's a gap filler. It's a placeholder.

In an incredible conversation with Zach Frank, head of people analytics at audiovisual services provider Freeman, we talked about the role of automation at work. One of the points he hammered home is that automation holds some value, but the **real** opportunity for value is in how the time savings is used.[74] See, if we automate something and free up an hour a week in our schedule, but then we fill that hour with meaningless activities, then that automation didn't really create any new value. However, if we use that time instead to build deeper skills, strengthen stakeholder relationships, or tackle longstanding challenges, then we've created new value as a result of that automation. *As you'll see in the case study at the end of this chapter, one automation company took a dose of its own medicine and reaped the benefits when*

122

it comes to employee onboarding.

I've found in my talks with thousands of HR and business leaders since 2020's global pandemic began that my mission isn't just to educate, it's to **inspire**. By now you have a wide variety of ideas, strategies, and practices that you can explore, experiment, and implement within your own role and company. But I want you to hear me loud and clear: **the future of the People function is more heavily aligned with technology than it's ever been in the past**.

In our research, we see what I call TEP, or technology-enabled performance. When you hear that, you might imagine doctors utilizing image scanners to identify cancer, supply chain experts using sensors that detect information and report back to a remote location, or people on a manufacturing floor using artificial intelligence to spot potential safety hazards. But the People function is also supported by technology.

Over and over again in my work and through countless conversations, I have run across leaders that leverage technology not just to automate an activity or support a process, but to actually drive the performance of their function. If or when they leave that company, one of the first calls they make upon landing at their new firm is to their preferred technology providers in order to bring them along to the new firm. I've informally called them "superfans," but it really comes down to the performance aspect. Imagine if I told you that tomorrow you had to give up email and go back to telegrams as your primary way of communicating at work. It's inconceivable.

Yet that same attachment to email and other common work tools extends to HR solutions.

- Recruiting leaders can't imagine not having an applicant tracking system or recruitment marketing tools to target specific candidate communications.
- Not a single learning professional in existence would rather go back to 100% instructor led training in person with a binder full of paper certificates to track completion records. A learning management system and learning experience tools can do that much easier.
- People leaders don't want to manually track payroll,

calculate overtime, or track time away from work. We have a variety of payroll, HRIS, and workforce management technologies to do that for us.

In one interview with a payroll company that targets nursing homes and elder care facilities, the team told me that whenever leadership at one of those organizations changes hands from someone over 50 years old to someone under 40 years old, there's almost always an immediate increase in the amount of technology those firms use. Younger workers and leaders don't just an affection for technology that drives those decisions—they have less tolerance for inefficient processes.

Technology-enabled performance. Today, we can get more things accomplished in less time. We can deliver higher quality interventions because we have better data. Sure, it feels like we're busier than ever in the HR profession, but that's also due to the fact that expectations are higher than ever. We can't do this through sheer human power alone.

Robotics, Generative AI, and Other Cutting-Edge Innovations

In the last year we've seen more interest in generative AI, or AI that can be used to create new/original content. In the fall of 2022, ChatGPT was on everyone's lips as people used the tool to answer common questions, create new content, and simply explore the limits of today's artificial intelligence applications. I was actually tagged on LinkedIn by a friend that used the algorithm to answer the question "who are the major influencers in HR?" because, to my surprise, my name showed up in the AI-generated response.

ChatGPT, by the way, is a technology developed by OpenAI to use natural language models to understand and answer questions in a very human way. The use cases are intriguing.

- Marketers can use it to generate copywriting and content
- Testing code for bugs or errors
- Answering customer questions and providing basic service

But not all is positive. Some question the ethics of using a system like this when it's pulling from human entries and creating something new—who owns that output? In fact, some professors are even catching students using the technology to create research papers.[75]

It's pretty easy to see that these tools are able to quickly automate some simple activities like rapid content generation for blog posts and articles, but content jobs aren't the only ones that might be affected. In a study released early in 2023, researchers found that the AI generation capabilities of ChatGPT were strong enough to pass the MBA exam at the University of Pennsylvania's Wharton School of Business, giving the professor running the study a surprise and level of concern about what this means for the future of such programs.[76] In addition, one company leader used ChatGPT to generate a job application that made it to the top 20% of candidates on the shortlist for consideration before he let his recruiting team know that they had been duped.[77]

There is a tremendous amount of interest in this area in the market. Companies like Jasper, Stability, and others are using large data sets to generate new content, and investors are pouring tons of money into these firms. Stability received $100 million as a seed round just to launch the company initially, which is unheard of for such an early-stage company.[78] I expect to see more of these kinds of stories as the public becomes more comfortable using systems like ChatGPT and others to explore the impact of artificial intelligence tools on work, education, and life.

In tangible terms, robotics is also playing a part in shaking up the world of work. Robots have been around for quite some time, and they continue to get smarter and more capable. Videos of Spot the robot dog opening doors on YouTube have been viewed tens of millions of times.[79] Apparently, we are all fascinated by the development and evolution of these technologies.

In a recent discussion with the HR executive in charge of the technologies used at a global logistics company, he explained that the firm recently began leveraging robots at many of their warehouses, but probably not in the way you might think. The company, like most enterprise logistics and warehousing firms, is using robots for picking and sorting packages and deliveries. However, it recently began using robots as sentries for security purposes. It leverages a combination of on-the-ground robots as well as flying drones to monitor and evaluate possible security issues.

The number of robots in use has ballooned in recent years, especially when the public was looking for "no touch" ways to interact with businesses during the pandemic.

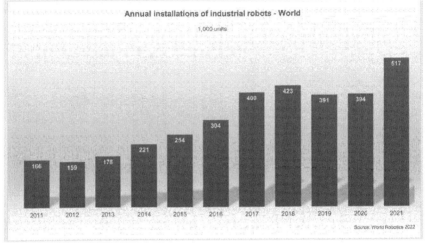

Annual installations of industrial robots - World

1,000 units

166	159	178	221	254	304	400	423	391	394	517
2011	2012	2013	2014	2015	2016	2017	2018	2019	2020	2021

Source: World Robotics 2022

Figure 7.2[80]

From a more consumer-focused lens, robotics equipment is being used in areas like food and beverage. There was fanfare when the Mezli "fully automated" restaurant opened in San Francisco in 2022.[81] The restaurant essentially serves as a sort of assembly line for food that has been partially prepared by a chef and other kitchen staff.

It breaks down like this: each morning, the kitchen staff prepare a menu of Mediterranean food at a kitchen and drops it off at the restaurant before it opens for the day. Customers enter and order on a digital screen, and food is then heated and assembled by the system before being deposited into a smart locker that can be unlocked by the customer after payment is received. The owners claim that the cost of building a Mezli is a fraction of the cost of building a new restaurant, and with no humans in the loop when it comes to serving the food, that minimizes the daily operating cost.

With many companies struggling to staff their restaurants sufficiently, this approach can clearly shrink the number of workers needed to run a food service operation. Regardless of how you feel about the experience of ordering and being served in an automated fashion, I wouldn't be surprised to see more of these types of concepts appearing around the globe.

I'll close with an example that may hit closer to home. Workplace health and safety today looks a lot like it did 30 years ago. Between posters and safety training, most of the elements haven't changed. But newer technologies like artificial intelligence are being used to help identify potential risks and flag them for action. CompScience is one of these companies, and as an example, one customer using this technology was able to save $300,000 on its insurance policy because of a 23% reduction in the injury rate for its workforce. Using existing video from work sites, the technology platform generates proprietary risk factors from 50+ behavioral and environmental unique hazard detectors through the use of computer vision. The system was designed from the ground up with privacy at the forefront: the AI-driven video analytics system does not identify individuals or retain personal information of any kind.

These varying examples help to show that a very diverse set of careers from worker's compensation jobs and security-related roles to restaurant positions like cashiers and food preparation are all seeing impacts from these technology advancements. These are just a small snippet of the many examples in place today across virtually every industry that exists.

In a world where talent scarcity is a reality, we should expect to see more of these types of technologies, both software and hardware, being used in and around the workplace. In these examples, the technologies are doing work that a human used to carry out.

Beyond the novelty factor, there is a tremendous amount of job-impacting change happening as well. In a new MIT study, researchers found that for every robot added per 1,000 U.S. workers, wages declined by 0.42% and the employment-to-population ratio reduced by 0.2%.[82] Specifically, the research found that adding a robot in a commuting zone reduced employment by six workers in the area. While some argue that new jobs will be created for the maintenance and repair of the robot workforce, it's unclear at this point how much that will offset the number of jobs lost and how many of those individuals losing jobs could be reskilled into another role.

But not all change is happening just from physical robots carrying out tasks. When you hear the term "robot," you probably imagine a physical machine. But robotic process automation is a type of software that automates repetitive tasks. Often called "swivel chair automation" because the tasks RPA completes are likened to a person entering information in one system, swiveling their chair around, and entering that information into another system. RPA can be used to enter duplicate data into multiple systems, keeping them synchronized. In the Zapier case study at the end of this chapter, we show how that team used its own software to automate elements of the onboarding process with RPA. While it sounds simple, RPA has a profound impact on the workplace. One study estimates that 800 million jobs will be impacted by RPA by 2030.[83]

Post-Automation: Targeting Top Performers

Let's acknowledge that in the big picture, even with automation becoming more and more common in the workplace, hiring and retention are going to be more important than ever. With fewer workers to go around, each of them will hold more value in the work they do. Put another way: when you have 1,000 staff, hiring 10 new ones will not dramatically change the direction of the company. When you have 50 staff, hiring 10 new ones can significantly shift the culture and direction of the firm. With more automation taking over jobs, companies will have fewer people in certain roles. We're trading off a higher volume or quantity of workers for fewer, higher quality ones.

That's a great sentiment, but when you add up all of the potential workers that exist, their average performance is, well, average. It's important to call out that the competition for high-performing workers will be extremely intense.

Let me illustrate with a fascinating study performed a few years back. A researcher gathered data from a wide variety of company founders and administered each of them a test of their innovativeness or creativity. He then plotted those results against the company's performance in the market (jobs created, revenue, etc.) The findings were clear: the most innovative founders had radically better results when compared against others in the study.[84]

I share this story because it's an example of what employers risk when they hire someone.

- Does every individual we hire have the same influence, insight, or capability as a company founder? Certainly not.
- Is there still a difference in the results and impact from a high performer versus a low performer? You better believe it.

There has been an ebb and flow around the quality of hire discussion over the years. When hiring is fast and frenzied, we're less focused on quality of hire. When hiring slows and is more deliberate, we're more focused on it. In a talent scarcity environment, quality will be paramount.

Think of it this way: in early 2022, companies were hiring as fast as possible to fill a wide variety of positions. If you had a job open and interviewed with two great candidates, you had to make the right decision about who to select the first time. With the pace of the market, you wouldn't get a second chance to make an offer to the silver medalist that didn't get chosen, because in most cases they would have already accepted another job.

Speaking of job offers, companies will need ways to identify who is likely to be a top performer in the hiring process or perhaps even before that. With quality workers in demand, having a way to identify a high-performing individual before they even apply would allow the company to market directly to those individuals over time, creating a warm foundation for an actual job offer conversation. In addition, companies will similarly need to find ways to measure and identify the performance of existing staff. We can't base performance solely on someone's likability. We need to know that they are able to achieve the tasks and goals the position requires. Assessments and other tools already exist for some of these use cases, and employers that are using them are already reducing their risk when it comes to hiring, performance, and retention.

Case Study: How Zapier Automated 86 Weeks' Worth of Onboarding

Zapier is an automation company. It's what the entire team does. They build and support integrations between hundreds of different software tools, enabling businesses to automate data retrieval and other activities. For instance, when someone submits a form on a website, Zapier can send that form data to a sales system and also add the person to a spreadsheet list for follow up contact. Or when a new video is published on a YouTube channel, Zapier can trigger a blog post and a social media notification. The automation combinations are nearly limitless.

But when the company's onboarding expert Ashley Priebe Brown started, Zapier's onboarding looked nothing like the external company's image led her to believe. It was full of manual tasks, activities, and processes that were clunky, inefficient, and labor-intensive. New hires were pulled in a dozen different directions every day for their first few weeks, often leading to a more stressful experience than intended.

Ashley and the team began revising the approach and focusing or "chunking" content that was related into different sections so that there were fewer transitions for new hires in their early days, as the image below shows. There was a section of live/synchronous sessions with team members and others, but there was also a healthy dose of asynchronous (self-paced) activities as well to provide opportunities for experiential learning and growth.[85]

Zapier Onboarding Flow
(Days 1-3 only)

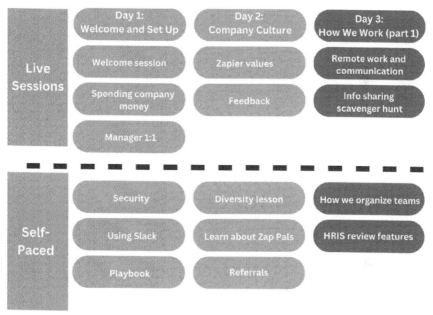

Figure 7.3

Ultimately, the onboarding team was able to use automations and smarter design processes to reduce 86 weeks of time spent by the team previously on manual activities related to onboarding. This included everything from setting up dozens of calendar invites to sending routine information and more. By taking these steps to automate, the team was able to then move into more strategic solutions like process design, evaluating new hire feedback, and other priorities.

8

CHANGE, AGILITY, AND
RESETTING EXPECTATIONS

Think about the dozens of things you do daily without much thought. You tie your shoes, brush your teeth, or even drive your car with minimal attention given to the task. Our brains are conditioned to streamline common, ordinary tasks to eliminate decisions and conserve energy. But occasionally something happens that shocks us out of our reverie. Years ago, a professor was getting dressed absentmindedly. In the middle of the process, he stopped and realized he'd been trying to button his vest for at least a minute with no success. He looked down and realized that his daughter had sewn the buttonholes closed[86].

In a moment of clarity, he saw this very visual example that our brains will continue on with a task, even if it's fruitless, until we consciously take over and make an intentional decision about what to do next. That "autopilot" or "muscle memory" approach to things is handy and helpful in everyday situations, because without it we would be mentally exhausted just a few hours into the day if we had to make every decision consciously. Imagine having to tell your body how to balance when you stand up, when to move each foot when walking, and so on!

What do buttonholes have to do with work? Well, it's a great parallel to how we make decisions in a business context daily. If we want a more modern or complex version of this concept, let's look at heuristics. Put simply, heuristics are about using previous experiences with problems to define how we approach future problems of similar structure and content. When programmers are teaching antivirus software to identify new computer viruses, they teach it using the structure of previous viruses. Using heuristics, it can identify a virus, even if it's not an exact match of old virus code, and it does so because it identifies a similar structure or command within the program.

Every day, business leaders use that same process to make decisions about how to solve problems using their collective experiences, intuition, and (hopefully) data. When a new problem comes, they pattern match against previous problems to identify common elements before selecting a path forward. However, when a new or different problem arises, it's much more difficult to pattern match and determine the best course of action. In the case of a talent shortage, the majority of business leaders just haven't had to deal with that issue in the past, so it's a new and different challenge.

One way I recently described this in a recent keynote presentation was by quickly summarizing the history of manufacturing practices. In the early days, it was common to stockpile large sources of raw materials to produce goods. However, when logistics and transportation improved to a predictable degree, business leaders turned to the practice of just in time manufacturing, where they only stockpiled the amount of raw materials and inventory necessary to operate for a short period of time. This allowed them to free up cash and space. However, when supply chain disruptions hit, just in time practices quickly stalled out. Those of us who watched the toilet paper shortage unfold during the early days of COVID know what that fallout can look like.

Shortages, Skills, and Adaptability

From 2020 until 2022, for instance, there was a global shortage of computer chips needed to produce electronic goods, including automotive goods. At one point, there were tens of thousands of nearly complete vehicles sitting in parking lots across the United States waiting for computer chips to finalize assembly and be ready for service.[87]

I'm bringing these examples to the forefront because they are a reminder that even when something works really well, there comes a time when it gets upended. In the case of talent and hiring, we have always assumed that the just in time approach works there, too. When someone leaves, we can post a position and find other people available to fill it. However, as the last few years have shown, that isn't always the case. There are some industries with seemingly perpetual shortages, like nursing and trucking. Those industries have talked about those challenges for years, and while there have been some attempts to correct or mitigate the issues, they still exist and, in some cases, have gotten even worse.

What will we do, then, when those shortages come to other types of roles that we need to maintain business operations? What will we do when we run out of accountants, supply chain professionals, or biomedical researchers? No profession is immune to this. Recently, a People Operations leader told me about a shortage of teachers in his area. The local school district was trying to create new incentives and relocation packages to bring teachers into the area because there weren't enough to fill local positions. If this shortage hit just one area or another, businesses, communities, and nations could create feeder programs to drive talent into those fields with incentives and/or higher pay. But when it cuts across every field in a true shortage, it can't be solved that easily.

A skills model first mentioned all the way back in 1991 may factor into this. Called the "T-shape" model, it looks at individuals with a depth of skills in one area but a broad set of knowledge for the base.

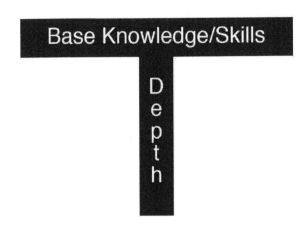

T-Shaped Person

Figure 8.1

This model was helpful when work was less dynamic, because that depth served people well. However, in a change-rich environment, T-shaped individuals may not be as flexible, which is why the "Key-shaped" skills model began to emerge.

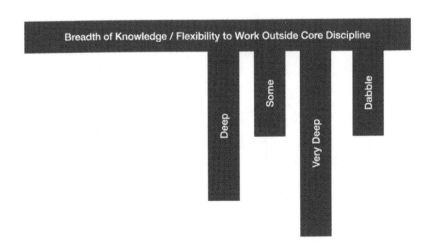

Key-Shaped Person

Figure 8.2

This model assumes that same base of knowledge across multiple areas, but a set of differing levels of expertise in several different areas. The pace and scope of change aren't the only things affecting this transition in skills focus. There's also the element of wicked learning environments. In kind environments, we learn quickly from our actions and their consequences and are able to adjust quickly.[88] A few characteristics of kind learning environments:

- Receive quick feedback on our actions and their effectiveness
- Understand all of the rules and constraints in any particular situation
- Have a high degree of predictability in situations and outcomes

As you can probably tell, that sounds more like a lab experiment than real life. Based on those criteria, work is a wicked learning environment for sure. We often have random, unpredictable situations or circumstances. We get feedback that is biased, late, or fragmented, when we even get feedback at all. And there are often no two situations that are exactly the same from which we can learn and adapt.

In those situations, someone who is very deep in only one area is challenged heavily because they lack other domain knowledge to apply when the situation doesn't match their specific area of expertise. Having even a bit of depth in other areas makes any one of us more change-resistant and flexible in the face of difficult and unexpected situations, both in work and in life.

To apply this to the specific skills shortage conversation, we could probably survive a shortage of accountants if we have enough operations, supply chain, or marketing leaders who understand how to budget, allocate funds, and so forth. While some types of expertise are deep and difficult to replicate (pediatric neurosurgeons, for example), this kind of multiskilled approach can afford us some flexibility as an overall workforce. The problem is that we don't always reward or encourage this breadth even though we should.

In the last HR practitioner job I held, I worked for an incredible leader. I reported directly to the CEO, and one of his common sayings in leadership team meetings was "tell me how we can, not why we can't." His background in Special Forces aviation may have had something to do with that sentiment, because nearly every mission was a life-or-death scenario. While the stakes were lower in our daily work, there was still an expectation that we wouldn't quit without exploring every possible option and alternative. It wasn't uncommon to have a meeting where finance, contracts, or even human resources was sharing about a situation and offering several possible alternatives to consider. This sentiment is one that I hope all of us can cling to in our daily work. While there are some situations with no good options, there are many more situations where options exist if we are willing to look hard enough.

Matching Workforce Depletion with Hiring Strategies

Throughout this book we have looked at the numerous reasons people leave the workplace, and we've also examined some of the strategies and opportunities for them to stay. I don't want to assume that you are connecting every dot, so I have added a table below that aligns strategies and case studies with some of the drivers of talent scarcity.

Affected Workers	Talent Strategy	Story or Case Study
Older workers	• Targeted hiring campaigns	EasyJet, AlliedUniversal, CVS
	• Phased retirement	Aerospace Corporation, CVS
Caregivers	• Returnships	Audible
	• Flexible work schedules	Manufacturing "parent shift" story
Women	• Flexible work schedules	Manufacturing "parent shift" story
	• Boomerang campaigns	Aerospace firm targeting working mothers
Entrepreneurs and gig workers	• Opportunities to innovate within	Coca Cola, *USS Santa Fe*
	• Hackathons	ADTRAN
Shortages of key personnel	• Innovative hiring and retention strategies	Healthcare international hiring story
		Nussbaum Trucking retention

		story

This isn't an exhaustive list, but it helps to demonstrate that if we diligently seek out a solution to a problem, there's likely to be a way to respond and react in a positive way. Our data show over and over again that companies are able to mitigate or overcome challenges when they can pivot in an agile way.

Business Agility is More Than a Buzzword

In the past few years, the word "unprecedented" has been used more than any other. It's becoming so commonplace that I recently saw the term "permacrisis" used to describe what seems to be the perpetual state of crisis and change that the headlines point to on a regular basis. Things have changed, sure, but the one thing that has stayed the same is the need for leaders who are able to think in an agile way. Business agility has never been more important, and those of us who can quickly adapt and change will be able to respond more quickly to those changing circumstances.

This demand for agility has been highlighted in recent years. NEOMA, a French business school, has co-produced research on agility and their definition is a great one: agility is an organization's ability to make timely, effective, and sustained changes resulting in performance advantages.[89] Our own definition that we use at Lighthouse is similar: agility is an organizational capability focusing on being able to adapt to changing conditions and challenges as they arise.

In a 2020 study of workplace agility across 1,000 enterprise employers, our team found that 97% of human resources leaders believe that the technology they use to hire, manage, and support their workforce helps to make the company more agile and responsive to change.[90] Logically that makes sense. The tools we use to support our largest and most valuable resource, our people, **should** play a part in our agility as a business. That study indicated that elements that we might take for granted, like the user experience for employees or enabling workforce productivity are key contributors to that agility. Conversely, a lack of critical features and an HR technology stack that isn't unified both limit agility. But while our People technology has an impact, there's more to business agility to be considered, as the following examples illustrate.

Three Examples of Business Pivots

Pivoting a business is hard. In the textbooks, every business starts with a well-crafted business plan that examines market needs and how the business can solve it. In truth, many businesses start with a dream. Someone begins solving a market need because they also had that need at one time. I find that story over and over again in the HR technology industry: a compensation startup that was founded by a leader who faced pay equity issues, a hiring technology founder who was treated like a number instead of a person, or a training technology company that was started by a person who was pass over for promotions and development opportunities.

But a dream can't sustain a business forever. It needs to solve a real problem in a meaningful way at an acceptable price. In the following examples, companies made that transition and have become names that we're all familiar with. I share these stories because they illustrate how ideas for pivots can come from internal staff, external users, or from unique circumstances that are hard to predict. In a world of talent scarcity, we're all going to have to pivot to some degree to adjust to what comes next.

One of the world's largest and most well-known makers of video games is the Japanese company Nintendo. Nearly everyone knows the company's characters from its first hit games: Donkey Kong and Super Mario, but did you know that Nintendo was founded in 1889 as a maker of Japanese playing cards? There were ups and downs in the following years with varying successes, but in 1953 Nintendo was the first Japanese company to successfully mass produce playing cards.[91] A partnership with Disney in 1959 meant Nintendo was focused heavily on the children's market, selling millions of cards and expanding into producing board games in addition to cards.

Then it all began to change. With the Disney partnership, Nintendo was heavily dependent on the children's market to maintain the company's growth and success. Additionally, with adult interest in Japan shifting to other sports like bowling, sales of its other cards began to taper off. And when the Disney card sales began to slow, Nintendo's leadership realized that it was in danger.

The period between 1965 and the 1980s saw Nintendo's leadership trying idea after idea to try and keep the company afloat. Arcade games, electronic toys, and other tabletop games were all produced in an attempt to find Nintendo's niche in the world. Finally, the company's games and its Nintendo Entertainment System were launched in the U.S. in 1985, thus beginning a long and successful run at producing both games and devices for operating those. From the original Game Boy handheld game launched in 1989 to the Wii in 2006 to the Nintendo Switch in 2017, the company has continued to meet and exceed expectations for casual and dedicated gamers alike.

This pivot example is one where the company saw its one key revenue stream drying up, leading to a new strategy and approach. This happened with the original cards, the shift to children's cards and games, and again when console games were threatened by handheld devices. Knowing customers and using their inputs to help shape what and how you deliver as a business is a critical success factor for those businesses that stand the test of time.

A shorter and more direct story comes from Kutol. This is a company name that virtually nobody recognizes, yet most of us have held their product in our hands at one time or another.

Kutol was a company that primarily made soap, but we know it for the product launched in the 1930s as a cleaning agent. In those days, many homes in the U.S. had coal-fired furnaces, which left black soot and residue on the walls (and wallpaper) nearby. One day in the late 1920s, a sales representative was visiting a Kroger store and was asked by the manager if he sold anything that might remove those soot stains safely. It was a common customer request, and none of the products in stock were designed for that purpose. The sales representative quickly said that his company had a solution for that and sold 15,000 cases of the stuff to Kroger. The problem? The product didn't actually exist. After some trial and error, the man and his brother found a way to develop this cleaning agent and began selling it to other stores and locations.

Kutol was designed to remove that soot in a way that was safe for wallpaper, which couldn't get wet. However, in the following years, more and more homes began to use gas and electric heat, and the demand for coal residue cleaners fell precipitously.[92] As the company's leaders looked for ways to survive, a preschool teacher showed up to save the day.

She had been looking for cheap materials to use for a class project and purchased some of the wallpaper cleaning compound. Seeing how much the children in her class loved playing with it, she called the company and told them that they should consider selling it as a toy, offering up her recommendation for a potential name: Play-Doh.

Since that pivotal moment, millions of cans of this colorful child's toy have been sold, leading to happy children and creating fun memories that would have never been associated with a simple cleaning solution.

We could use countless stories here to continue down this path, but hopefully you're getting the picture. When circumstances change, we have to find ways to change and evolve with them, or we disappear. Would someone else be likely to eventually create a sort of child's play toy if Kutol hadn't? Absolutely. But all of the knockoffs and other similar products don't have the name recognition and trusted brand that Play-Doh has established over the years. A key part of its early success was capitalizing on the relationships with schools where it sold its soap prior. Those schools and their many students were a fertile ground for the new Play-Doh offering.

Maybe I gravitated to these examples because my own kids love these things, but I'll share one more that's a little less child-focused.

If you visited Seattle in 1971, you could visit a small store in town to purchase internationally sourced coffee beans, tea, and spices to use at home. Many customers did, and this was a fairly successful business for many years.

However, in 1983, one of the company's employees visited Italy. On that trip, he experienced the hospitality and warmth of the country's well-known coffeehouses, deciding to bring that same atmosphere back to his home country. When that employee, Howard Schultz, returned home, he began the process of shifting Starbucks into what we know it as today.[93] Instead of being the place where you buy your own beans or tea leaves, you can get a custom cup of coffee, espresso, or other drink made to order. As the model transitioned, Starbucks began expanding to other cities and states like Chicago and California, filling millions of cups of coffee and becoming a billion-dollar company over time. Today, the company has more than 30,000 stores worldwide.

I won't belabor the history and other aspects of the journey for the most well-known coffeehouse in the world, but this pivot is different from the others. Starbucks wasn't in trouble or on the verge of failure. It was doing something and doing it well. However, there was a gap in the U.S. market that Schultz saw in his international travels, and that awareness and realization is what triggered the change in direction to the Starbucks we all know today.

Sometimes the pivot is driven by changing market conditions (Nintendo). Sometimes it's driven by customer inputs and ideas (Play-Doh). And sometimes it's driven by a new or innovative idea that nobody else had considered and executed sufficiently (Starbucks).

This isn't a book specifically about business pivots, but if we're going to experience a shift of some kind in the availability of talent, we need to be ready to adjust. Even in a talent shortage, or perhaps **especially** in one, we need to consider new ideas and alternatives like never before.

I'll close with this reiteration of a key statistic from our research with a little modifier attached. In 2022, more than eight in 10 talent leaders told us that hiring and retention conversations rose from an HR/recruiting level discussion to a business/operational level discussion, cutting across hierarchies and requiring a more strategic look at talent. But we saw an interesting breakdown in how companies responded to that question.

Firms who we identify as Talent-Centric, those companies that put talent at the heart of their business decisions, were about 30%

more likely to agree with that statement about talent as a business priority than those who were not talent-centered.

For years, one of the common approaches in business was "customer first." There's absolutely nothing wrong with serving customers and serving them well, but increasingly we are finding employers that take an "employee first" approach. Those firms understand the connection between the workforce and business impact clearly.

- Supporting the workforce means they will take care of customers, going the extra mile when the occasion calls for it.
- Satisfied customers will purchase more, return more frequently, and refer others to the business.
- Increased sales and profitability means the organization can attract and retain more talent, continuing the virtuous cycle.

Figure 8.3

The question to ask is whether your organization is going to be Talent-Centric or not. This doesn't happen by accident, but thankfully you've received dozens of inputs, ideas, and real examples within the pages of this book to help you develop a business where talent isn't a "necessary evil" to getting things done, but a necessary foundation for building a world-class organization in every possible way.

Case Study: Using Hackathons for Engagement and Innovation at ADTRAN

ADTRAN is a 2,000-employee engineering firm headquartered in Cummings Research Park, one of the largest research parks in the United States. ADTRAN also has offices in Germany and India. The company is known in its hometown of Huntsville, Alabama for its innovation, and the staff credits its continued innovation in part to the hackathons and the type of culture those activities promote.

The hackathons are events "by engineers, for engineers," according to May Chen, an engineer at the company. This was a grassroots program launched by three of the firm's 400+ engineering staff, but support goes all the way to the top. Chen, one of the leaders of the initiative, said "We've had tremendous support. Business, IT, strategy, R&D–all the business units believe in what we're doing." This concept of ownership and self-leadership was echoed by the company's marketing leader: "This is definitely organically steered. Leaders stay out of hackathon management and leave it to the engineering staff."

And while hackathons also happen as community events in many locations across the world, there is something special about having this happen within the walls of the company. Kaley Schweikart, Human Resource Leader – Americas, explained, "This lets them do these internally instead of outside. It helps the workers and us as a company to grow and foster an innovative and creative team and culture."

Figure 8.4

The celebration wall, shown here within ADTRAN headquarters, displays its many patents and serves as a testament to the firm's culture of innovation.

In 2013, the hackathon movement inside the organization started very slowly. To launch the program, the team needed to get buy-in from the firm's leadership. R&D wasn't fully on board with the idea of hackathons initially. After all, it's a significant investment of resource costs. Workers spend approximately one day coding and working and half a day presenting and demoing their solution. One of the initial negotiation points for launching the hackathons was that they must be business related, but this later changed when the value of the events became clear. By 2014, the hackathon events were a standard practice within the company.

Today, there is an incredible amount of excitement among the employee base for the regularly scheduled hackathons to occur. The events are consistently growing in terms of participation rate, and recent events have had between 70 and 100 participants out of an engineering population of 400-500 workers. Additionally, the events have picked up in interest from those outside engineering, widening the participating audience to include IT, marketing, user experience, manufacturing, and other areas of the business.

Because this is a business exercise, not just a day off work, the outputs from the hackathon matter. To look at this from a practical angle, outsiders often wonder what sorts of outcomes result from the investment in a hackathon. For the team at ADTRAN, there are numerous outputs both tangible and intangible. Tangible results have come from multiple events:

- One proof of concept reduced processing time for a work activity by an order of magnitude, greatly improving productivity.
- Another was teaching engineers a new programming language by creating simple applications using the specific target language.
- A critical development from one session was the virtual test bed, a solution that allows the engineering team to simulate hardware and software usage without requiring thousands of dollars of actual hardware installations.

On the intangible side, one of the key benefits is allowing participants to leverage skills and strengths they might not use in their daily workflow, such as project management skills or more specific technical skills related to a task or process. Additional value points from a human capital perspective are explored in the section below on unintended benefits.

From a logistical perspective, Hackathon events currently happen on a regular cycle at ADTRAN. Three times a year the firm dedicates a day and a half to the internal hackathon, enabling workers to focus on other projects and innovations that might fall outside the scope of their daily work.

The committee starts with a training workshop for people unfamiliar with the themed topic. In this session they offer participants a use case and tools to use. Additionally, for those engineers that don't have a dedicated project they want to pursue, "seed" projects can be provided for those new to hackathons to help ease them into the process.

What follows is a fairly intense day-long dive into the team projects. Engineers work in focused bursts over eight to 10 hours to make as much progress as possible in the dedicated time slot. Their end goal? Presenting a five-to-eight-minute presentation about their project in hopes of getting it funded. The actual presentation time, while short, gives each a chance to explain the concept, show off any models or prototypes, and then comes the fun part: teams are subject to unlimited Q&A time to allow participants the opportunity to ask questions, dissect ideas, and fully grasp the concept and its impact.

This "demo day" takes place the day immediately after the workers have hacked their specific area of focus. The only requirement for participating in the hackathon is that the team must also participate in demo day to show off their work. The company sees this as a combination of springboard for new ideas that the workers can't get to in their day-to-day as well as an opportunity to explore new technology.

The intended and unintended consequences and value are important metrics for any company wanting to follow in ADTRAN footsteps. While these events were started with the hope of driving creativity and innovation among the engineering population, the company's leaders quickly realized there were some unforeseen benefits to creating this type of initiative. For instance, the VP of HR for the Americas, Kaley Schweikart, mentioned that the company couldn't have used advertising or other media as effectively as the word-of-mouth that results from the innovative culture the firm has created. She credits the success of the ongoing college co-op engineering program in part to the hackathons. The firm funnels around 160 co-op students through its engineering department each year.

Additionally, the Vice President of Marketing, Gary Bolton, confirmed that the hackathons were a key differentiator in the hiring process. Recruiters talk about the events with candidates as a way to demonstrate the unique culture of the firm, branding ADTRAN as a fast-paced innovator, which some might not expect from a 30+ year old firm.

When competing with high-tech firms like Google and Facebook for software developer talent, employers like ADTRAN can use hackathons to stand out competitively from an employer branding perspective.

Plus, with a greater focus on skills acquisition in today's workplace, the hackathon events provide a powerful way to not only teach a new skill, but also offer an immediate opportunity to apply it in practice. For instance, the advent of more artificial intelligence and machine learning technologies in the marketplace has the engineers hungry for skills and knowledge on those topics. In a recent AI-themed hackathon (the topic was voted on by the engineering staff, not dictated by company leadership), the group used a short, structured learning workshop to educate workers on the basics of AI/ML, then they were encouraged to put those new learning concepts into practice by developing a program or improvement using those ideas.

Sjohn Chambers, one of the company's engineers, explained, "We have this hackathon culture internally. For the last three years, I've really hated if I had to miss a hackathon for some reason. The engineers all look forward to this." In addition to the specific process of hacking, Chambers also said this is woven into his own performance review process. "The hackathon projects and results are a part of my performance reviews and my own career development. My manager and I have these kinds of discussions regularly."

Additionally, the team told me the magnetic pull of the innovative culture was so strong that one employee that left the company for another engineering firm ended up coming back because he missed the hackathons. This story, while anecdotal, shows that the other engineers that are still with the firm are there due in part to this specific practice. It has a powerful influence not just on bringing workers in but in keeping them engaged.

More broadly, ADTRAN is the largest patent holder in Alabama. The company has 60% more patents per R&D dollar invested than the industry average, and more than 21% of revenue goes into R&D on a regular basis to keep the innovation at the front of the market. In the image above you can see the company's internal wall dedicated to the patents it holds. For a company dedicated to improving its innovation and innovative capabilities, there is no higher honor than that level of recognition.

The final step in any hackathon is the AAR—After Action Review. Obviously the team hopes that each hackathon event will bring creative new ideas to the forefront, but it doesn't take that for granted. The three organizers and the hackathon committee of eight engineers gather for an AAR to dissect each event and understand what worked and what didn't. This retrospective offers valuable insights.

Sjohn Chambers, one of the participating engineers, said, "Honestly you can learn as much if it fails as if it succeeds. Not all projects are 'successful,' and success is relative."

As a team, the members ask questions in the review about what was learned, what went wrong, and what went right. In addition, time is spent on exploring what to change for the next session to improve it even further. Despite having several years of hackathons under their belt, the team is still learning, a testament to the culture of continuous improvement and innovation.

Case Study: Identifying Points of Failure and Driving Flexibility at Motley Fool

The Motley Fool is a financial services company headquartered in the United States. The company began as an investment services and advisory firm and continues today, but the firm has some unique approaches to how it manages employees. One of those eccentricities is the "Fool's Errand."

Every month during the company all-hands meeting, one person's name is drawn from a hat at random. That individual must take a spontaneous vacation immediately with no company contact for two consecutive weeks. The winner of this drawing receives $1,500 to spend however they choose in addition to their time away from the office.

This is positioned by the company as a benefit, and it's true that any of us would appreciate a check for $1,500 and two paid weeks off. But there's another aspect to this that is perhaps even more valuable on the company side, and that's ensuring team continuity.

At any time, any team member could end up sick or out of work for any reason, and for many companies, this can be a time of crisis and tension. The Motley Fool is tackling this problem a little bit at a time by ensuring that random person is unable to communicate for that two-week period, ensuring that the team is able to operate without a single point of failure.

While this approach is likely too adventurous for most of us, the lesson it teaches is a good one: there's always the possibility that someone will be out of work for an extended time. If we practice for that, we'll be able to adapt more quickly if and when that unexpected moment does happen.

---

[73] https://www.shopify.com/enterprise/why-seth-godin-wrote-a-book-for-people-who-dont-usually-read-books

[74] https://onlyhumanshow.com/e/the-one-thing-people-analytics-teams-often-get-wrong/

[75] https://futurism.com/college-student-caught-writing-paper-chatgpt

[76] https://www.nbcnews.com/tech/tech-news/chatgpt-passes-mba-exam-wharton-professor-rcna67036

[77] https://www.yahoo.com/now/business-owner-had-chatgpt-apply-200821433.html?guccounter=1&guce_referrer=aHR0cHM6Ly93d3cuZ29vZ2xlLmNvbS8&guce_referrer_sig=AQAAAHoHqc5NcHyAUWqnMAxQCfQHZRt_ZkimUMisWWO5G0Mpr_fB1Er-umxbjJtEQqeGMjF53Y48nv0Ep-IC4gHZtJOmMaJ7F_q71DkiP5AaaamWvPxNGSRynjtJ31A-d3xiyFKZz0Jl2BZYyLgilLA31wV8_hui0vClSUUBBas-ok9w

[78] https://secrets.thestarrconspiracy.com/generative-ai-for-generative-growth

[79] https://www.youtube.com/watch?v=wXxrmussq4E

[80] https://agfundernews.com/robotics-use-growing-at-breathtaking-speed-as-food-bev-industry-automation-increases-25-ifr-report#:~:text=There%20are%20now%20over%20500%2C000,slump%20in%202019%20and%202020.

[81] https://www.restaurant-hospitality.com/technology/world-s-first-completely-automated-restaurant

[82] https://mitsloan.mit.edu/ideas-made-to-matter/a-new-study-measures-actual-impact-robots-jobs-its-significant

[83] https://www.bbc.com/news/world-us-canada-42170100

[84] https://www.academia.edu/25926533/Personal_innovativeness_as_a_predictor_of_entrepreneurial_value_creation

[85] https://zapier.com/blog/how-zapier-automates-onboarding/

[86] *I Dare You (1967)*

[87] https://www.motortrend.com/news/chip-shortage-gm-unfinished-vehicles/

[88] https://www.psychologytoday.com/us/blog/experience-studio/202007/experience-kind-vs-wicked

[89] https://neoma-bs.com/news/what-is-the-link-between-agility-and-performance/

[90] https://lhra.io/blog/is-there-a-relationship-between-hr-technology-and-organizational-agility-new-research/

[91] https://www.nintendo.co.jp/corporate/en/history/index.html

[92] https://www.businessinsider.com/the-shocking-story-behind-playdohs-original-purpose-2015-9

[93] https://www.starbucks.com/about-us/

Afterword

One of the pains of writing a book like this is seeing the perfect moment pass by. If my time machine was in working order, I'd have released this book early in 2022 as the world's hiring activity neared a frenzied point. At the time of this writing as the book wraps up for publication, the hiring pressure is still on in some ways, but the technology industry has laid off a number of workers at the same time, and it's an uncertain period for a lot of employers and workers.

Those circumstances don't change the words, data, and ideas shared in the previous pages. All of the indicators show that we're at the front end of what will be a challenging hiring environment at minimum and an earth-shattering scenario at worst. This may be a short lull or an extended one, but only time will tell.

Regardless, I appreciate the time, attention, and effort it takes to consume a book about such a weighty topic. I hope you picked up some ideas and insights that help you think more critically about hiring and keeping your workforce both now and in the future. If you want more information about the topic or to see some of my ongoing research, you can learn more at the TalentScarcity.com website.

References

Every attempt has been made to include and incorporate references to other material as accurately and comprehensively as possible. For ease of consumption, the endnotes for each chapter include links that were live and valid at the time of publication.

Made in the USA
Columbia, SC
09 February 2023

11780301R00093